Apple Pro Training Series
Shake 3

Marco Paolini

Apple
Certified

Apple Pro Training Series: Shake 3
Marco Paolini
Copyright © 2004 by Digital Film Tools, LLC

Published by Peachpit Press. For information on Peachpit Press books, contact:

Peachpit Press
1249 Eighth Street
Berkeley, CA 94710
(510) 524-2178
Fax: (510) 524-2221
http://www.peachpit.com
To report errors, please send a note to errata@peachpit.com
Peachpit Press is a division of Pearson Education

Editor: Serena Herr
Production Editor: Connie Jeung-Mills
Project Editor: Anita Dennis
Technical Editor: Damian Allen
Copy Editor: Darren Meiss
Interior design: Frances Baca
Compositor: Maureen Forys, Happenstance Type-O-Rama
Indexer: Karin Arrigoni
Cover design and illustration: Frances Baca

ISBN 0-321-19725-9
9 8 7 6 5 4 3 2
Printed and bound in the United States of America

To who else—Mom and Dad

Acknowledgements When I was asked to write this book, I severely underestimated the time it would take to accomplish the task. To the responsible parties, thank you for getting me into this; I hope one day to return the favor. To everybody who had to put up with me throughout the writing of this book, I apologize. To those who kept me on track and guided me along the way, thanks.

Peter Warner Thanks for allowing me to adapt some of your tutorials and documentation.

Peter Moyer Thanks for providing high-quality footage as well as writing the original Advanced Compositing lesson.

Ed Quirk Thanks for providing the majority of the swank, 3D computer-generated imagery throughout the book. If it looks good, Ed did it.

Louis Cetorelli Thanks for giving me the opportunity to write the original Shake training materials and answering my endless stream of stupid questions.

Patty Montesion Thanks for asking me to write this book.

Peachpit Press Thanks to the entire team at Peachpit Press who did all of the thankless, behind-the-scenes production of this book.

My wife and kids Thanks for putting up with me.

Contents at a Glance

Table of Contents

Getting Started

The leading compositing system for feature film effects, Shake™ from Apple is a high-speed compositing software optimized for high-resolution visual effects. Designed for quality, speed, and efficiency, Shake has quickly become the leading compositing choice for cutting-edge visual effects in feature films, as well as IMAX films. Since its debut, Shake has been used in every film that won the Academy Award for Visual Effects—*Titanic, What Dreams May Come, The Matrix, Gladiator, The Lord of the Rings: The Fellowship of the Ring,* and *Lord of the Rings: The Two Towers.*

About Apple Pro Training Series

Apple Pro Training Series Shake 3 is part of the official training series for Apple graphics, editing, and authoring software developed by experts in the field. The lessons are designed to let you learn at your own pace. If you're new to Shake, you'll learn the fundamental concepts and features you'll need to master the program. If you've been using Shake for a while, you'll find that this book teaches many advanced features, including tips and techniques for using the latest version of Shake.

Although each lesson provides step-by-step instructions for creating a specific project, there's room for exploration and experimentation. I recommend that you follow the book from start to finish, or at least complete the first five chapters before jumping around in a haphazard manner. Each lesson concludes with a review section summarizing what you've learned.

System Requirements

Before beginning to use *Apple Pro Training Series Shake 3*, you should have a working knowledge of your computer and its operating system. Make sure that you know how to use the mouse and standard menus and commands and also how to open, save, and close files. If you need to review these techniques, see the printed or online documentation included with your system.

Before you install Shake, ensure that your system meets the following minimum requirements:

Macintosh System Configuration

Minimum Desktop Hardware and Software Configuration

- 800 MHz PowerPC G4 or higher desktop
- Mac OS X 10.2.5 (or later)
- Three-button mouse
- QuickTime 6.0 (or later)

- 1GB local disk space for caching and temporary files
- 256MB of RAM
- A video display card with 32MB of VRAM and Open GL hardware acceleration, such as the NVIDIA® 4 MX™ or ATI® Radeon™ 7500
- 1280 × 1024 display with 24-bit color

Minimum PowerBook Hardware and Software Configuration

- 800 MHz PowerPC G4 or higher PowerBook
- Mac OS X 10.2.5 (or later)
- Three-button mouse
- QuickTime 6.0 (or later)
- 1GB local disk space for caching and temporary files
- 256MB of RAM
- A video display card with 32MB of VRAM and Open GL hardware acceleration, such as the NVIDIA®4 MX™ or ATI® Radeon™ 7500
- 1280 × 1024 display with 24-bit color (optional for external monitor)

Minimum Server Hardware and Software Configuration

- 1 GHz PowerPC G4 or higher XServe
- Mac OS X Server 10.2.5 (or later)
- Three-button mouse (optional for render station, required for compositing seat)
- QuickTime 6.0 (or later)
- 1GB local disk space for caching and temporary files
- 256MB of RAM
- A video display card with 32MB of VRAM and Open GL hardware acceleration, such as the NVIDIA® 4 MX™ or ATI® Radeon™ 7500 (optional for render station, required for compositing seat)
- 1280 × 1024 display with 24-bit color (optional for render station, required for compositing seat)

Installing Shake

The DVD that accompanies this book includes a full copy of Shake 3. A free 30-day license is available online. Use the following guidelines to install and start Shake on a Macintosh OS X 10.2.5 system.

> **NOTE** ► Shake requires you to use Mac OS X 10.2.5 (or later). If you do not have Mac OS X 10.2.5, you need to install it on your system before you can run Shake.

Installing Shake on a Macintosh System

This installation will require you to restart your computer. We recommend you close all applications before starting to install.

1   Insert the *Apple Pro Training Series Shake 3* DVD into your DVD drive.

2   Go to the Trial Software folder and copy the **Shake3.dmg** file to your desktop.

3   Double-click the **Shake3.dmg** file.

    The Shake3 volume is created.

4   Double-click the Shake3 volume icon.

    The Install Shake 3 icon appears in the Shake3 window.

5   Double-click the Shake 3 icon.

    The Install Shake and Authenticate windows appear.

6   In the Authenticate window, enter your Mac OS X Name and Password or phrase.

7   In the Install Shake window, follow the onscreen instructions.

Destination Options

In the Select Destination dialog, installation is only available on partitions with Mac OS X 10.2.5 (or later). By default, Shake is installed in the Applications folder on your hard drive. Although the Applications folder is the recommended folder, you can move Shake to a different folder.

Installation Options

In the Installation Type dialog, select one of the following installation options:

- **Upgrade**—Performs an Easy Install, which includes Shake and the documentation, but no tutorial images
- **Customize**—Gives you the option to install Shake and the documentation, only the tutorial images, or Shake and the documentation with the tutorial images

Shake Folder Contents

When Shake is installed, four icons appear in the Shake3 folder: Shake, shkqtv, shkv, and a doc folder. The Shake icon represents the Shake application, and it can be placed in the Dock. The shkv icon represents the Shake Viewer application (the flipbook player). You cannot launch the Shake Viewer application outside of Shake. When you create a flipbook in Shake, the Shake Viewer is automatically launched and the shkv icon appears in the Dock.

> **NOTE ▶** All of the Shake files are stored within the application. To view the Shake package contents, Ctrl-click / right-click the Shake icon and select Show Package Contents.

Obtaining the 30-Day Free License

Before you can launch Shake, you must obtain a license. This book comes with a free 30-day license of Shake, available online.

1   In your Web browser, go to http://shake.apple.com/shakedemo.

2   Follow the instructions to download and install your free license.

   NOTE ▶ Your 30-day license begins on the day you download it.

Copying the Shake Lesson Files

The *Apple Pro Training Series Shake 3* DVD includes folders containing all the electronic files for the lessons. Each lesson has its own folder. You must install these folders on your hard drive to use the files for the lessons. To save room on your drive, you can install the folders for each lesson as you need them.

Installing the Shake Lesson Files

1   Insert the *Apple Pro Training Series Shake 3* DVD into your DVD drive.

2   Create a folder on your hard drive and name it *Shake Lessons*.

3   Drag the Lessons folder from the DVD into the Shake Lessons folder on your hard drive.

Resources

This book is not meant to replace the documentation that comes with the program. Only the commands used in the lessons are explained in the book. For comprehensive information about program features, refer to these resources:

- The Reference Guide—Accessed through the Shake Help menu, the Reference Guide contains a complete description of all features.

- Tutorials—The Shake Help menu includes a useful set of tutorials.

- The Apple Web site—You can view the Web site by choosing Help > Shake Home Page if you have a connection to the World Wide Web, or go to www.apple.com/shake.

Apple Pro End-User Certification

The Apple Pro Training and Certification Programs are designed to keep you at the forefront of Apple's digital media technology while giving you a competitive edge in today's ever-changing job market. Whether you're an editor, graphic designer, sound designer, special effects artist, or teacher, these training tools are meant to help you expand your skills.

Upon completing the course material in this book, you can become an Apple Pro by taking the certification exam at an Apple Authorized Training Center. Certification is offered in Final Cut Pro 4 (two levels), DVD Studio Pro 2, Shake 3, and Logic 6. Successful certification as an Apple Pro gives you official recognition of your knowledge of Apple's professional applications while allowing you to market yourself to employers and clients as a skilled, pro-level user of Apple products.

To find an Authorized Training Center near you, go to www.apple.com/software/pro/training.

For those who prefer to learn in an instructor-led setting, Apple also offers training courses at Apple Authorized Training Centers worldwide. These courses, which use the Apple Pro Training Series books as their curriculum, are taught by Apple Certified Trainers and balance concepts and lectures with hands-on labs and exercises. Apple Authorized Training Centers for Pro products have been carefully selected and have met Apple's highest standards in all areas, including facilities, instructors, course delivery, and infrastructure. The goal of the program is to offer Apple customers, from beginners to the most seasoned professionals, the highest quality training experience.

1

Lesson Files	Lessons > Lesson01 folder
Media	fairy.1-50.iff
Time	approximately 45 minutes
Goals	Start the Shake software
	Demonstrate the Shake interface
	Import images and sequences
	Use the Viewer to play back images

The Shake Workflow

Shake is a collection of image manipulation engines, such as compositing, color correction, or warping engines. Each engine can be driven by a series of different commands called (interchangeably) nodes or processes. For example, Brightness is a node to change the brightness of an image; Pan is a node that moves the image left and right and up and down. Each node usually has a series of parameters (or values) that can be adjusted. These nodes are connected to images and arranged in what is called a process tree because, well, it kind of looks like a tree.

The interesting thing about Shake is that the nodes and their parameters can be edited either in the interface (graphical user interface, or GUI) or from the command line in a Terminal window. It makes no difference to the composite how these nodes are executed from Shake, but each method has its advantages or disadvantages in terms of workflow. Shake's command line functions are covered in Lesson 14.

Interface Workflow

- Images are read in from various folders.

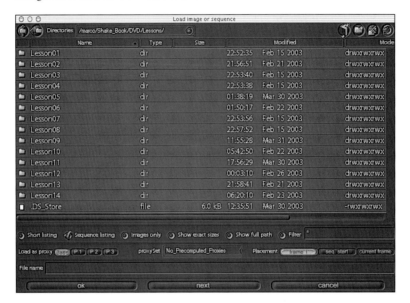

- These images, as represented by the thumbnails, are arranged in a compositing tree, with color corrections, layering commands, and keying nodes, among others, connected to them to achieve the desired effect.

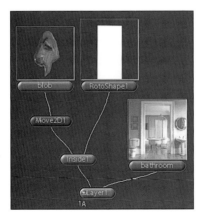

- The parameters of the nodes are tuned with interactive feedback in the viewing windows.

- Once finished, a FileOut node is attached to the bottom of the compositing tree to tell Shake where to write the output image.

You can use as many FileOuts as you want, placed anywhere along the tree. You can render from the interface by choosing FileOut, and then selecting Render FileOut Nodes in the Render menu.

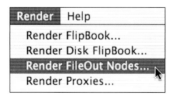

- Or you can save the tree out as a text file called a Shake script.

```
blob.shk
// Shake v3.00.0325 - (c) Apple Computer, Inc. 1998-2003.  All Rights Reserved.
// Apple, the Apple logo, Shake, and Tremor are trademarks of Apple Computer, Inc.,
registered in the U.S. and other countries.
// Primatte 20 (c) Photron Ltd. 2002
// FLEXlm 8.1b (c) Globetrotter Software 2002. Globetrotter and FLEXlm are registered
trademarks of Macrovision Corporation.


SetTimeRange("1-46");
SetFieldRendering(0);
SetFps(24);
SetMotionBlur(1, 1, 0);
SetQuality(1);
SetUseProxy("Base");
SetProxyFilter("default");
SetPixelScale(1, 1);
SetUseProxyOnMissing(1);
SetDefaultWidth(720);
SetDefaultHeight(486);
SetDefaultBytes(1);
SetDefaultAspect(1);
SetDefaultViewerAspect(1);
SetTimecodeMode("24 FPS");

DefineProxyPath("No_Precomputed_Proxy", 1, 1, -1, "Auto", -1, 0, 0, "",1);
DefineProxyPath("No_Precomputed_Proxy", 0.5, 1, 1, "Auto", 0, 0, 1, "");
DefineProxyPath("No_Precomputed_Proxy", 0.25, 1, 1, "Auto", 0, 0, 2, "");
DefineProxyPath("No_Precomputed_Proxy", 0.1, 1, 1, "Auto", 0, 0, 3, "");
SetAudio("100W@E0000qFdsuHW962DI9BOW0mWa06w7mCJ000000000008");

// Input nodes
```

- From the Terminal window or your own batch rendering system, the effect is then rendered, and the output image is written to disk.

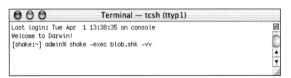

```
Terminal — tcsh (ttyp1)
Last login: Tue Apr  1 13:38:35 on console
Welcome to Darwin!
[shake:~] admin% shake -exec blob.shk -vv
```

The Shake Interface

The time has come. You've just installed the Shake software; now you get to see it in action. Before you start working with the various Shake processes, you should become familiar with the Shake interface.

1   If you don't have a three-button mouse, go and buy one now.

   NOTE ▶ You must have a three-button mouse to operate Shake properly.

2 Turn on your computer and monitor.

The login screen will appear in a moment.

3 Type your name and password at the login prompt.

4 Launch Shake by double-clicking on the Shake icon located in your Applications/Shake folder.

NOTE ▶ You may want to create an alias of the Shake icon on your desktop.

After you launch Shake, you should see something that looks like this, but without the silly numbers:

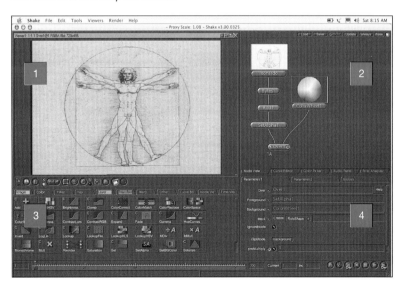

By default, Shake has four main workspaces:

1. The Viewer workspace, or Node View

2. The Node workspace

3. The Tool tabs

4. The Parameters workspace

    You can resize the four quadrants at any time by clicking and dragging on the horizontal or vertical dividing lines of any two areas.

    Click on the dividing line between the Parameters workspace and the Tool tabs and drag left and right to change the layout of the Shake interface.

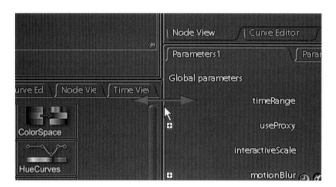

The Viewer Workspace

The Viewer workspace is where you create flipbooks to play back your images. This is also where your images and composites are interactively updated as you add nodes and change parameters. Here, you can look at the Red, Green, Blue, or Alpha components of an image. You can zoom in or out as well as create split screens to look at before and afters.

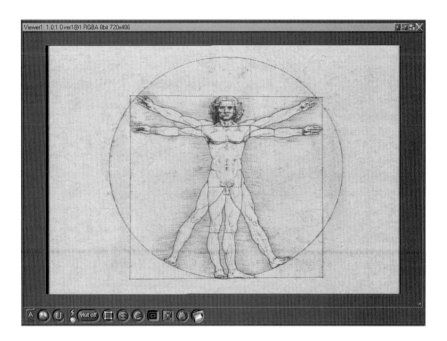

The Tool Tabs

The Tool tabs allow you to choose what node you want to add to your process tree. Each node serves a particular function, such as color correction, image filtering, or layering. The nodes are logically placed into different tabs according to their functions.

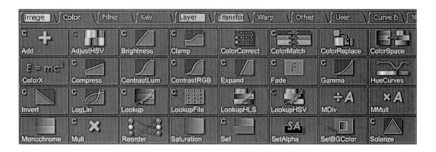

The Tool tabs are made up of the following tabs:

- Image
- Color
- Filter
- Key
- Layer
- Transform

- Warp
- Other
- Curve Editor
- Node View
- Time View

The Parameters Workspace

Adjustments made to a node's parameters take place inside of the Parameters workspace. Clicking on the right side of a node will place that node's particular set of controls into the Parameters workspace. You can adjust parameters by moving sliders, typing values, or entering expressions.

Global parameters are adjusted from within the Parameters workspace by clicking on the Globals tab. These parameters affect the behavior of your entire effect setup, or what Shake refers to as a script, setting things like the time range and global motion blur controls. You can set many of these parameters in the command line, so you don't necessarily have to reset them each time you write out a script.

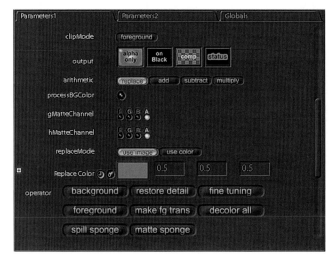

Primatte node loaded into Parameters workspace

The Node Workspace

The Node workspace is where you work with the many and varied process nodes. This is where the magic happens. Clips and processes are combined and together they form a Shake script. The script can be saved, loaded, and reused at a later time. The script is also referred to as a process tree, or just tree, because when all of the clips and processes are hooked together it looks like a tree (not a very healthy one, but a tree nevertheless).

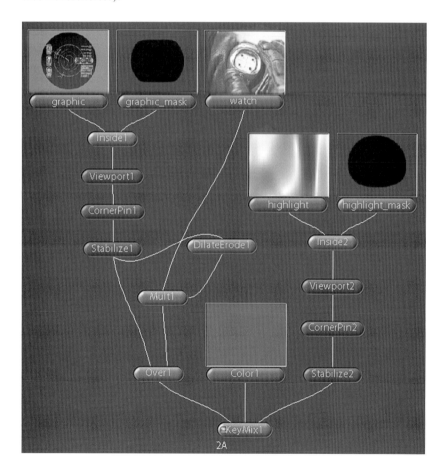

2A

Color Picker

The color picker allows you to sample colors from the Viewer and transfer the color settings to applicable parameters. It can be found on a tab on the Node workspace.

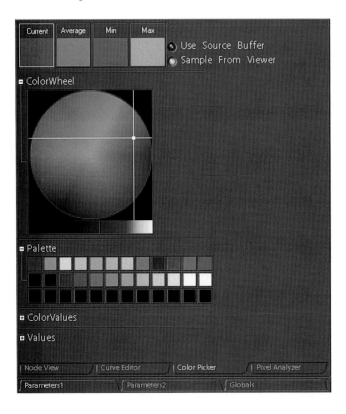

Pixel Analyzer

The Pixel Analyzer is an analysis tool used to find and compare different color values of an image. You can examine mimimum, average, current, or maximum pixel values on a selection or across an entire image. It's found on the Pixel Analyzer tab in the Node workspace.

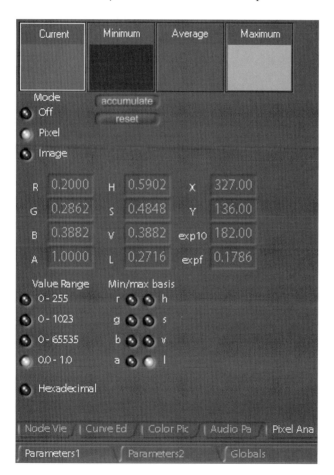

Time View

The Time View tab shows a timeline of all clips and processes within a
script. You can drag a clip left and right to change its start and end points
in time or drag its in/out points to change its duration.

Curve Editor

The Curve Editor allows you to create, see, and modify keyframes as well
as animation curves and audio waveforms. You can change the curve type,
as well as its cycling mode. You can access the Curve Editor through the
Tool tabs as well as on the Node workspace.

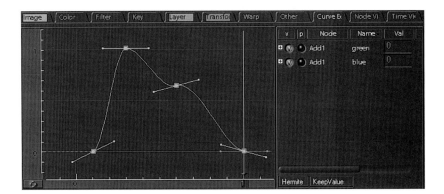

Audio Panel

The Audio Panel is used to read in AIFF or WAV files, mix them together, extract animation curves based on the audio frequency, manipulate the timing of the sound, and save the files again. Click the Audio Panel tab on the Node workspace to access it.

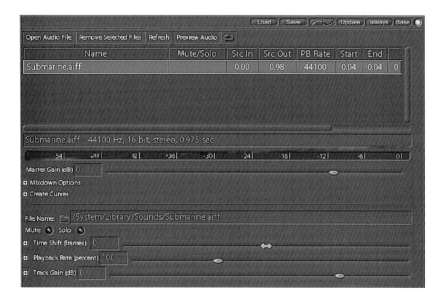

Title Bar Functions

- **Pull-down menus**

A series of pull-down menus is located at the top-left portion of the screen. Many common functions such as script loading and saving can be accessed through these menus.

- **Render light**

When the light is green, Shake isn't processing. When the light is red, it is. The cursor also changes to indicate processing.

· **Load/Save**

Clicking on the Load/Save buttons calls up the browser to either load a script or to save the current script with the same name. To save a script under a new name, choose File > Save As, which will then prompt you for a script name. To reload the same script, choose File > Reload. This will reload the script that you see on the Shake title bar.

NOTE ▶ Remember that these buttons apply only to the loading and saving of scripts and not to the loading of media into Shake.

· **Infinite undo/redo buttons**

By saving changes into temporary files, Shake maintains infinite undo/redo. Not all changes are flagged as "undo-able," though. For example, window sizes are not saved. The left arrow button performs the undo; the right arrow button does a redo.

You can also press Cmd-Z to undo and Cmd-Y to redo.

· **Update buttons**

The Update button has three modes that can be seen in a drop-down menu. The menu appears when you click and hold the left mouse button on the Always button.

- **Always**

  Shake always updates the scene when you change a parameter, including time.

- **Manual**

  Shake never updates the scene, including time, until you click Update, the button on the left.

- **Release**

  Shake updates the scene when you release the mouse after changing any parameter, including time.

  The Update button is used to manually update the scene when the Update mode is set to Manual.

- **Proxy buttons**

  A proxy is a lower resolution copy that you substitute for your high-resolution images so that you can work faster. The proxy buttons activate the use of proxy resolutions. When this is set to the Base position, it turns off the use of proxy images.

- **Title bar information**

  The title bar of the Shake window gives you current version data, as well as the current script name and the current proxy resolution.

  ⊖ ⊖ ⊖   Shake_Book/DVD/Lessons/Lesson12/scripts/watch.shk – Proxy Scale: 1.00 – Shake v3.00.0325

Contextual Help

Because most people will never read the Shake documentation, the Shake programmers have provided a contextual help window. As you pass the cursor over a button, the help window gives you a brief message about the button's function, as well as its hot key. The help information is located in the text window at the bottom center of the interface.

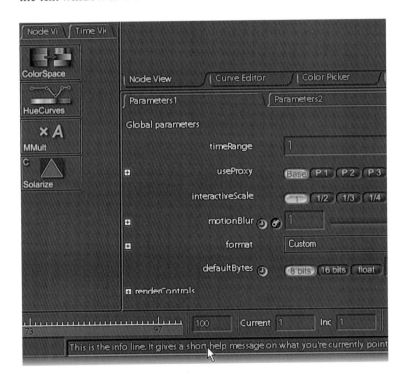

Node Help

Each Shake node has a Help button across from the name of the node—
the very first parameter listed in the Parameters tab. Click on the Help
button to open up your current default browser and a help explanation for
that particular node.

Online Documentation

For those rare souls who are actually interested in referring to the Shake
documentation, you can access it by selecting Help > Reference Guide. A
PDF reader will open showing the Shake documentation.

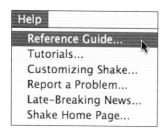

Importing Images and Sequences

Reading in an Image with the Browser

1 Drag the left mouse button along the Tool tabs (Image, Color, Filter, and so
   on) to see all of the function nodes you can insert into a compositing tree.

   Notice how you can just drag the mouse; you don't have to click on
   each tab to open it up.

2 To read in an image, you use the FileIn node in the Image tab. Click
   on it, and it will launch the file browser.

The browser is used whenever you are loading or saving images or reading and writing scripts.

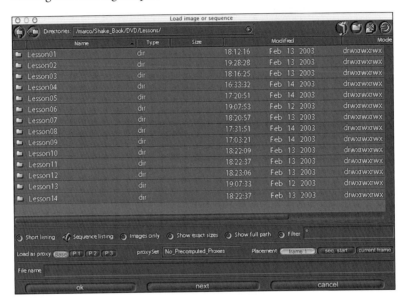

For this node, you will load the **fairy** clip, which is located inside the Lesson01 folder.

Browser Icons

There are six icons located at the top of the file browser. They are listed below for your reference.

Keystroke	Action
	go up one folder level
	go back to the previous folder
	bookmark the current folder
	create a new folder
	delete files/folders
	refresh a folder listing

3   Double-click on the Lesson01 folder.

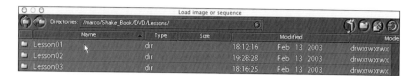

When you enter the Lesson01 folder, you'll see one sequence listed.

4   Click on **fairy.1-50#.iff** to select it.

5   Clicking OK creates a FileIn node in the Node View, and the image is loaded into the Viewer.

TIP ▶ When doing a FileIn, you can click OK to confirm and exit, or click Next to read in another file. Use Shift-click combinations to select multiple files.

In the Viewer, you should see an image of a photo-realistic fairy (I'm joking), and in the Node workspace, you should see one node named fairy.

6   Drag the mouse along the Time Bar at the bottom of the screen to see the frames update in the Viewer.

General Windowing

If you press the spacebar, you expand any workspace to fill the Shake screen.

1   Place the cursor over the Viewer and press the spacebar.

   The Viewer workspace expands to the entire desktop.

2   Press the spacebar again to go back to the normal view.

   Click the middle mouse button or Option-left-click to pan any workspace.

3   Pan the Viewer by Option-left-clicking.

   Some workspaces, such as Parameters, only scroll up and down.

Using the Viewer

This section gets you up to speed on using the Viewer.

General Viewer Controls

Now that you have something to look at, I can explain a bit about the Viewer workspace. The Viewer workspace is the area where you view your images, create flipbooks, and evaluate your composites. You can create as many Viewers as you want, each dynamically being updated in any channel you choose to any node you choose. This means that you can watch the behavior of a function as it modifies an alpha mask in both a Viewer looking at the alpha mask and a second Viewer looking at the composite itself.

The Viewers take up memory, so if you are doing a render, you might want to close your higher-resolution Viewers. Additionally, the more Viewers you have active, the slower the display rate will be. If you are getting strange Viewer behavior, free up some memory by deleting the Viewers and create a new one by pressing the N key.

1   Experiment with some of the general window controls in the Viewer:

   ▶   Iconify the Viewer.

   ▶   Fit Viewer to image (or press Ctrl-F).

   ▶   Fit Viewer to Desktop (or press Shift-F).

   ▶   Close window.

▶ Fit Image to Viewer (or press F)—This may result in non-integer zooming; for example, not zoomed x2, but x2.01, which may cause inaccuracies in the display of the image due to inherent rounding off of pixel rows.

▶ Reset Viewer Zoom and Pan to default (Home)—You can also press the Home key. This centers and sets zoom to a 1:1 ratio.

▶ Broadcast Monitor—When selected, the broadcast monitor mirrors the selected node—the node displayed in the Viewer. Prior to selecting this button, you should first choose your footage format from the Globals: format parameter.

2 Drag the mouse while pressing the left mouse button in the image area to see X, Y, R, G, B, and Alpha values in the help field and the title bar.

Viewer1: 1.0:1 fairy@1 RGBA 8bit 500x500 X=257 Y=315 R=0.365 G=0.306 B=0.259 A=1.000

3 Toggle the Channel Viewer using the left mouse button.

The Channel Viewer toggles between the full color image and the alpha channel. You can view the individual channels by first placing your cursor over the image area and pressing the R, G, B, A, and C keys to toggle between the red, green, blue, alpha and RGB view planes. If you have limited brain capacity and can't remember those five keystrokes, click and hold your left mouse button over the Channel Viewer to make your selection.

TIP Channel Viewer hot key: The 2 key cycles through the channels R, G, B, A, and RGB. Pressing 2 toggles forward, Shift-2 toggles backwards. The cursor must be in the Viewer window for this to work.

4 Press N ("new" Viewer) when the cursor is over the Viewer to clone it.

5 Place the cursor over the Viewer again and press the spacebar.

   This expands the Viewer workspace to full screen so that it is easier to view both Viewers.

6 Place your cursor over each Viewer and press Ctrl-F to fit the Viewer to the image.

7 On one of the Viewers, toggle the Channel Viewer to the alpha channel, or you can just press A.

You can move a Viewer around by grabbing its title bar. You can also resize it by grabbing its borders. You can have as many Viewers as you want, and each is "live," assuming that the Update mode is not set to No Update (see the following section).

Viewer Update Modes

When you create a Viewer, it is assigned to the active node, so the Viewer will show something new every time you create a new node or click to evaluate a different node. To create a new Viewer window, choose Viewers > New Viewer.

NOTE ▶ You can lock a Viewer to a node by double-clicking on a Viewer and then clicking on the node you want. Once you have assigned a Viewer to a specific node, you should create another Viewer to take the duty of viewing the active node.

1 Move the Time Bar, and you can see that both Viewers update.

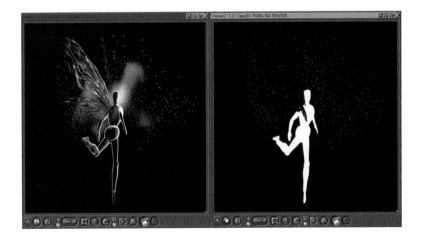

2   Try out the different Update modes in conjunction with moving the Time Bar. Click and hold on the Update icon with the left mouse button and then select any of the three Viewer Update modes.

▶   Normal update mode; image is presented when frame render is finished.

▶   Scrolling update mode; image is presented as it is rendered, scrolling upwards. Use this when you have large images and slow updates.

▶   No update mode; no update until toggled to Normal mode.

To kill the update of a Viewer, press the Esc key.

TIP   The number 3 cycles the Update mode. Pressing the 3 key toggles forward and Shift-3 toggles backwards. The cursor must be in the Viewer window for this to work.

3   Make sure the Update mode is returned to Normal.

4   Close the second Viewer that's showing the alpha channel and move the remaining Viewer to the bottom-left corner of the screen.

5   Press the spacebar to return the Viewer workspace to normal size.

6   Place your cursor over the Viewer and press Shift-F to fit the Viewer
     to the Desktop.

     Now, you should be back to normal.

Comparing Images

If you want to compare two different images or two different planes
within the same image, you can use the Compare buttons on the Viewer.
In this example, you will compare the RGB planes with the alpha plane.
The A and B tabs on the bottom left of the Viewer allow you to switch
between two images.

1   Make sure the A tab is on top and click on the left side of the fairy
     node in the Node View.

NOTE ▸ In case you were wondering, the 1A next to the node signi-
fies Viewer 1, Tab A.

This simply reloads the same image into the same Viewer and is therefore redundant.

2   Click once on the A tab to cycle it to the B tab.

3   Click on the left side of the fairy node again. This loads the same image into buffer B.

4   Press the A key with the cursor in the Viewer or toggle the Channel Viewer to the white dot icon to view the alpha channel.

5   You may have to click Home to center the image.

6   You can toggle the A and B tabs to compare the images.

TIP   The number 1 cycles the A and B tabs. Pressing the 1 key toggles forward, Shift-1 toggles backwards. The cursor must be in the Viewer window for this to work.

7   If you click and hold on the C at the bottom of the Viewer, you will see the Compare Sliders pop-up list.

8 Select the vertical compare slider.

9 Now grab the tiny little gray C icon in the lower-right corner of the Viewer and drag it left and right, revealing the two images.

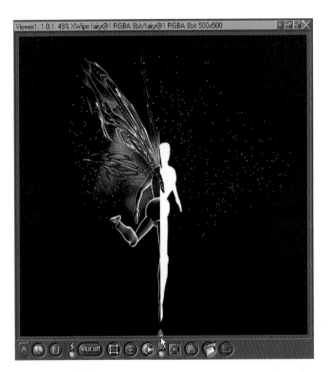

You can also use a horizontal or fading Compare mode.

TIP ▶ The number 5 cycles the Compare modes. Pressing the **5** key toggles forward, Ctrl-5 toggles backwards. The cursor must be in the Viewer window for this to work.

10 Return Compare to Normal mode.

NOTE ▶ Make sure you turn off the Compare mode before continuing, because you may accidentally leave the slider looking entirely at the B image when you are working on the A buffer image.

Creating Flipbooks to Play Back Clips

Can you just tell me how to play the darn clip already? All right, all right. To play the fairy clip, you need to create a flipbook. A flipbook is a RAM-based image player that loads a clip into memory, so that it can be played back in real time. The first step is to set the frame range.

1 Click on the Globals tab in the Parameters workspace.

This will load the Global parameters into the Parameters workspace.

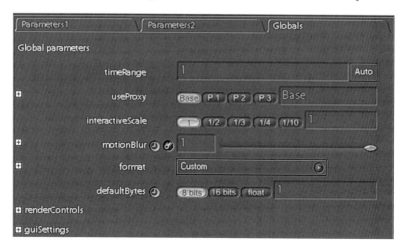

2 Under timeRange, enter *1-30* to load 30 frames.

1-30×2 means every other frame, 1-30×3 every third frame, and so on.

3 Now click the Flipbook icon at the bottom of the Viewer to launch a flipbook of your clip with the desired frame range.

> **TIP** If you press the right mouse button on the Flipbook icon, you can pop up a Render Parameters page to set your frame range and other settings. You can then set the frame range exactly as just described. Otherwise, it will use the Global settings you have set.

4 You can press the > key at any time while it is loading to see the clip play. Shake will continue to render and add frames in the background.

If you press stop (the spacebar) before it is done loading, you can continue the load by pressing / (the slash with the question mark) key. Given enough RAM, you can load as many flipbooks as you want.

5 Experiment with some of the flipbook shortcut keys listed at the end of this lesson.

6 When you are done playing around with the flipbook controls, close the flipbook by clicking on the X in the top-right corner of the flip-book window.

Congratulations! You made it through Lesson 1.

7 Exit Shake by choosing Shake > Quit Shake. Select No when prompted to save the script.

What You've Learned

- The Tool tabs display the various Shake processes.

- You use the FileIn node to import images and sequences.

- When you are done using the Compare mode, make sure you return to Normal mode so that you don't accidentally leave the slider looking at the B image when you are working on the A buffer image.

- You right-click on the Flipbook icon to set your frame range and other settings for a flipbook.

- You use the Viewer to play and view images.

Keyboard Shortcuts

Undo/Redo

Cmd-Z	undo
Cmd-Y	redo

General Windowing

Option-left mouse drag	pans window
Middle mouse drag	pans window
Spacebar	expands or collapses window
Ctrl-Option-drag	zooms some windows in and out (Curve Editor, Node View, Time Bar)
Ctrl-middle mouse drag	zooms some windows in and out (Curve Editor, Node View, Time Bar)
Esc	kills processing
U	updates Viewer

Keyboard Shortcuts (continued)

General Windowing

Shift-middle mouse drag on a tab	tears off a tab as a floating window (floating windows can be put back by simply closing them with the close button on the title bar)
Shift-Option-left mouse drag on a tab	tears off a tab as a floating window

Viewer

N	creates/copies new viewer
Ctrl-F	fits viewer to image
Shift-F	fits viewer to desktop
F	fits image to viewer
Option-drag	pans image
Home	resets viewer zoom and pan to default (Home)
R, G, B, A, C	toggles the red, green, blue, alpha, and RGB view planes
1	cycles the A/B tabs
2	cycles the R, G, B, A, and RGB view planes
3	cycles the Update modes
4	cycles the Viewer scripts
5	cycles the Compare modes
. (think of it as the > key)	plays forward
, (think of it as the < key)	plays backward

Keyboard Shortcuts (continued)

Flipbook

Shift-drag (in the flipbook windows)	scrubs clip
Right arrow key	advances frames
Left arrow key	steps back through frames
Spacebar	stops/plays clip or render
/	continues loading/render
Home	re-centers image
-/= (key next to Backspace)	zooms in and out
Keypad + or -	increases or decreases the playback frame rate
T	real-time toggle; drops frames in playback
R, G, B, A, C	views red/green/blue/alpha/color channels
H	if in Compare mode, sets to horizontal split
V	if in Compare mode, sets to vertical split
S	if in Compare mode, switches split
F	if in Compare mode, fades split
Esc	Closes flipbook

2

Lesson Files	Lessons > Lesson02 folder
Media	fish.1-50.rgb
	fish_bowl.1-50.rgb
	fish_comp.1-50.rgb
Time	approximately 45 minutes
Goals	Build a simple process tree
	Connect, rename, move, and delete nodes
	Edit parameters
	Demonstrate the premultiplication process
	Save and render an effect

Basic Compositing

Digital compositing is the seamless integration of multiple elements—elements which may come from vastly different sources. A successful composite may rely on many techniques, such as keying/matting, color correction, rotoscoping, and painting. At the end of the day, it's not what you did, but how the effect looks. Shake provides you with extensive tools to combine your elements into a seamless visual effect.

In this lesson you will composite two clips to create this scene.

Process Trees

Shake is composed of a collection of image manipulation engines—compositing, color correction, warping, and so on. Each engine can be driven by a series of different commands, called nodes or processes. These nodes are arranged into a treelike structure called a process tree. Shake saves a process tree into a file called a script. The terms "process tree" and "script" will be used interchangably throughout this book. Nodes can be added or inserted at any time, building up an effect in a nonlinear fashion. It is a very flexible way to create an effect, and it's easy to change. So your clients can endlessly noodle with their shots, and you can make changes quickly thanks to Shake's flexibility.

Creating a Simple Tree

This section walks you through the process of creating a simple tree.

Loading Images

Before creating a process tree, you need to load in some images:

1 Start Shake.

2 Go to the Image tab and select the FileIn node.

   The Image Browser will open up.

3 Navigate to the Lesson02 folder. You should see three sequences.

4 Select the first file, **fish.1-50#.rgb** and then click Next.

5 Repeat this process and FileIn the remaining two sequences: **fish_bowl.1-50#.rgb** and **fish_comp.1-50#.rgb**.

6 Close the FileIn browser when done.

TIP ► You can select a file or sequence from the browser in one step by double-clicking on it.

You now have three nodes in the Node View. They are named fish, fish_bowl and fish_comp—all named automatically by Shake. Since the parameters of the last node you created pop into the Parameters workspace automatically, you can see the fish_comp parameters listed in the bottom-right window.

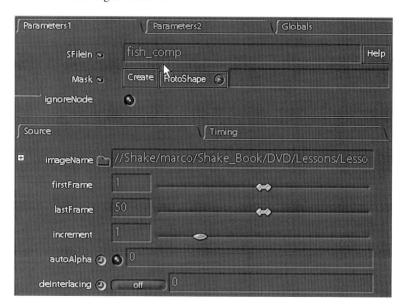

The first parameter shown is SFileIn, which should list fish_comp. If you want to rename the node, you can do so here. You can get the parameters of any node by clicking on that node's right side.

Click here to see an active node in the Viewer

Click here to see a node's parameters

If you double-click on the node, you simultaneously load the node into the active Viewer and list its parameters in the Parameters workspace. If you drag the cursor over the nodes, you see the node name, function type, and image information in the contextual help window at the bottom center of the Shake screen.

fish_comp (SFileIn) 8bit RGBA 720x486

7   Click on the left side of the fish_comp node to view the final shot.

You'll need to set the Global timeRange parameter, but instead of typing it manually, you can use the Auto button to do it for you.

8   Go to the Globals tab in the Parameters workspace.

9   To the right of the timeRange parameter, click on the Auto button.

The Auto button sets the time range to the length of the longest FileIn node. In this case, the range is set to 1-50.

10   Now click the Flipbook icon at the bottom of the Viewer, and it will launch a flipbook of your clip with the desired frame range.

11   Press the > key at any time while it is loading to see the clip play.

If you press stop (the spacebar) before it is done loading, you can continue the load by pressing / (the slash on the question mark key).

This is the final composite of the effect that you will be building.

The shot is the combination of a computer-generated fish and a live action fish tank. Your job will be to marry the two elements together so that it looks like one shot. First, take a look at each clip.

NOTE ▶ Whenever you are done playing a clip, close the flipbook window because it eats up precious RAM when left open.

12 Close the flipbook.

13 Repeat step 10 and load the **fish** and **fish_bowl** clips into flipbooks and play them.

The fish and fish_bowl nodes represent the two clips that need to be joined together.

14 Close all open flipbooks.

15 Double-click on the fish clip.

16 Toggle the Channel Viewer to the white dot icon to view the alpha channel.

The fish clip has an alpha channel that allows you to place the fish over the fish_bowl. It is basically a cookie cutter, and it is the heart of compositing. It just goes to show how simple compositing is. When you have an alpha channel, the white areas represent your foreground, and black areas represent your background in the final composite. Since the fish clip is a computer-generated element, a single click of a button creates and embeds the alpha channel into the clip during the rendering process.

17 Place your cursor over the Viewer and press the C key to view the RGB channels.

Attaching Nodes

You can insert nodes into a tree in one of five ways:

• By selecting the node you want under the Tools pull-down menu at the top of the screen.

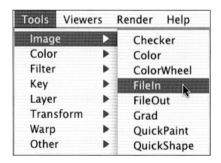

- By clicking the node in the Tool tabs in the bottom-left window of the Shake screen.

- By right-clicking the node in the Tool tabs in the bottom-left window of the Shake screen and selecting the method of insertion.

- By right-clicking on a Tool tab and selecting a node from the pop-up menu.

- By copying an existing node and pasting it. Cmd-C copies, Cmd-V pastes. You can also perform these functions by right-clicking in the Node workspace.

To start compositing, you need to attach a Layer node. Nodes are by default attached to the active node. Now this is important, so pay attention: The active node is the one highlighted in green.

1 Highlight the **fish** clip and click on the Over function in the Layer tab.

The Over node automatically attaches itself to the **fish** clip. Shake connects the output of the **fish** into the left input of the Over1 node. The Over function places one image over another according to the matte of the foreground image.

2 Attach the **fish_bowl** clip to the Over1 node. To do this, click on the output nub (this is the small dot that appears at the bottom of the node as you mouse over it) at the bottom of the fish_bowl node and drag to the right, or background, input of the Over1 node and release.

 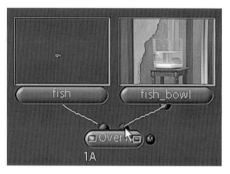

You should now see the **fish** and **fish_bowl** images composited as one. The color of the fish will need to be adjusted, but you'll do that in a moment.

NOTE ▶ The standard practice for layering operations that expect two input images is to connect the foreground to the first, or left, input and the background to the second, or right, input.

Premultiplication

For the Over node, the most frequently used Layer node, Shake assumes there is an alpha channel to determine the foreground pixels, and that the foreground image is premultiplied by that mask. Most computer-generated elements are generally always premultiplied. This includes the **fish** element.

Let's start by defining a premultiplied image: it is an image that has its RGB channels multiplied by its alpha channel. Typically, images rendered by 3D software are premultiplied, meaning the transparent areas have black both in the RGB areas and in the same areas of the alpha channel. A side effect of a premultiplied image is that the RGB channels never have a higher value than the alpha channel.

Scanned elements or other 2D-generated plates require an added alpha channel (also called the matte or mask channel), which is then used to premultiply that image with an optional setting in the Over node. To get that alpha channel, draw it with Shake's QuickPaint or RotoShape node or pull a key with Shake's keying functions. If the alpha channel is provided to you, read it in and then copy it into a foreground image's alpha channel with a SwitchMatte node. Once you premultiply, you can composite. For a more detailed explanation on premultiplication, refer to the Shake documentation.

Saving Your Tree

Before continuing, you should save your tree. Shake saves the tree as a script. A script is a text file that contains all of the information about your tree. The script can be loaded back into the interface for later work and can be rendered either from the Shake interface or from the command line.

> **TIP** To make your life easier, I have included a completed script for not only this lesson, but for all lessons. You can view these finished scripts in each lesson's scripts folder if you ever get stuck.

1 Select File > Save Script.

The browser will come up.

2 Create a new folder in your own Home directory to save your scripts and images. Navigate to your Home directory and click on the Create New Folder icon at the top right of the File Browser.

3 When prompted, type in *Shake_Output* for the name of the folder and click OK.

4 In the File name path, type *fish* for the name of your script and click OK.

Shake automatically puts a .shk extension at the end of your filename once it is saved.

NOTE ▶ If Shake were to crash and you hadn't saved your script, you could select File > Recover Script to recall the last autoSave script.

Inserting/Replacing/Creating Nodes

When you click on a tool in the tool tabs, that tool is inserted between the currently selected node (highlighted in green) and all of its children.

1 Click on the fish node so that it turns green, and from the Color tab, select Brightness.

A Brightness1 node is inserted between the fish node and the
Over1 node.

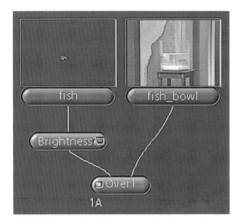

Right-clicking on any function in the tool tabs will give you four
different insertion choices for that particular node.

2 Right-click on the Gamma function from the Color tab and choose
Branch.

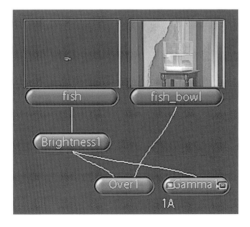

A new branch of the tree is created for the Gamma1 node off of the Brightness1 node.

3   With the Brightness1 node in your tree selected, right-click on the Compress function from the Color tab and select Replace.

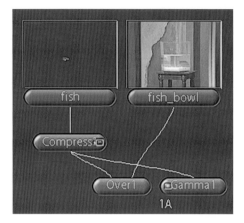

The Brightness1 node has been replaced by the Compress1 node.

4   Right-click on Add in the Color tab and choose Create.

A new unconnected Add1 node is added to the Node workspace.

You may have noticed when right-clicking a node in the tool tabs that each node insertion option has associated keyboard shortcuts. The keyboard shortcuts are listed at the end of this lesson for your reference.

Selecting Nodes

There are various ways to select and deselect nodes. Here are some of them:

1   Click-drag over the fish, Compress1, and Over1 nodes to select them. If you click-drag a selection box over any node in the Node View, the node becomes selected.

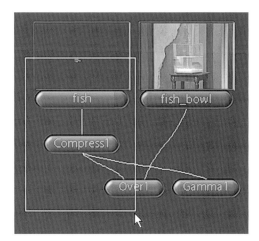

2   Ctrl-drag over the fish and Compress1 nodes to deselect them. If
    you Ctrl-drag over previously selected nodes on the Node View, you
    deselect them.

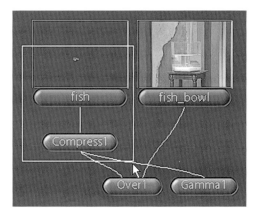

3   Press Cmd-A to select all nodes.

4   Click on the background area to deselect all nodes.

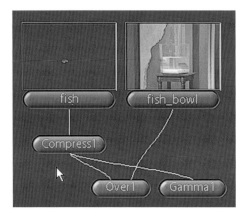

If you right-click on the Node workspace, you'll see quite a few other tree selection options along with their keyboard shortcuts.

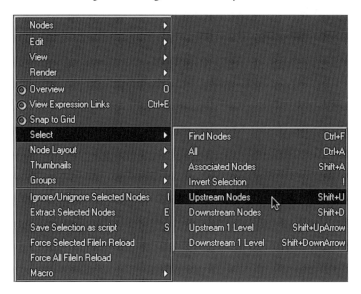

Detaching and Deleting Nodes

To delete a connection, put the cursor over the noodle (the connecting line) until it turns red or yellow and press the Macintosh Del key that is grouped with Home, Page Up, and Page Down on a full-sized keyboard. On Macintosh laptops, pressing the Fn and Delete keys simultaneously is the equivalent of the Del key.

> **NOTE ▶** On Linux and Irix systems, use the Delete key to carry out delete operations.

1   Place the cursor over the noodle connecting Mult1 to Gamma1 and press the Del key.

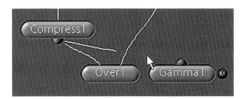

To delete nodes, select them and press the Del key.

2   Click on the Gamma1 node and press the Del key.

3   Click on the Add1 node and press the Del key.

Organizing Nodes

For those of you who like to keep your closets as well as your Node work-space tidy, Shake provides several node organizational features:

• Grab active nodes to drag them around.

• To organize all nodes, deselect all nodes and press L, for layout.

• To organize specific nodes, select the nodes and press L.

Editing Parameters

Before continuing, make sure your tree looks like this:

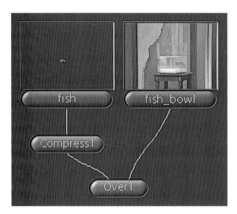

The composite is almost done, but the color of the fish is not quite matched. The Compress color function, which squeezes the image to fit within a Lo and Hi range that you set, is going to take care of this for you. It's a nifty way to modify the color of an image.

1   Click on the left side of the Over1 node to see it in the Viewer.

2   Click on the right side of the Compress1 node to bring its parameters into the Parameters workspace.

This configuration will allow you to view one node while editing the parameters of another. Without the capability to separately view and edit nodes, it would be like blowing down a West Texas country road at midnight. That's bad, real bad. The Compress1 node has red, green, blue and alpha parameters for both the Low and High ranges of the image. Click on the + to the left of the Low Color parameter.

3   Click on the + next to the R button.

4   Click in the number field for rLo, type in *.45*, and press Enter.

What the #$%? The whole image brightened up and not just the fish as expected. That's because you have just broken a most important rule: Don't color correct premultiplied images. If you color correct a premultiplied image, you can have problems with edges or with global levels being raised. Many people see this type of error and assume it is a mask problem, so they make the mask smaller in an attempt to get rid of the edge. Heathens! Happily, these problems are easily solved through proper management of premultiplication, which, I know, I haven't explained yet.

To solve this dilemma, you must first add an MDiv (Matte Divide) node from the Color tab to divide the **fish** image by its matte. This undoes the premultiplication. Second, you must activate the premultiply parameter in the Over node. You are then free to color correct to your heart's content.

5 Highlight the fish node and select an MDiv node from the Color tab.

6 Double-click on the Over1 node to select it and activate premultiply.

It's looking a bit better now.

7 Click on the right side of the Compress1 node to edit its parameters.

8 Click in the number field for gLo, type in .3, and press Enter.

But wait, there's more. Instead of typing a value into a field, we can do a little drag and drop. You can drag a parameter from one field to another by clicking on the parameter name and dragging it to the parameter name you want. This will copy from A to B.

9 Click on the gLo parameter name and drag and release on the bLo parameter name.

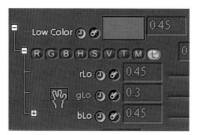

When you click on the green parameter name, a mutant three-fingered hand appears and then disappears when you release the mouse over the bLo parameter name. The value from gLo is transferred to the bLo parameter.

You can also create a link from B to A by pressing Shift when you drag and drop. Shift-click on parameter name A and drag to B; B will then be linked to A. Also, if you drag a collapsed parameter containing sub-parameters, all subparameters will be dragged as well.

10 Shift-click on the gLo parameter name and drag and release on the bLo parameter name.

A + sign appears to the left of the bLo parameter.

11 Click on the + to the left of the bLo parameter.

The expression bar opens and NRiScript1.Compress1.gLo is listed as an expression for the bLo parameter. This is called parameter linking and can be done not only within a node, but between other nodes in your tree. Parameter linking is covered in more detail in Lesson 12. Shake does some parameter linking for you within various nodes; you can tell this by the + sign next to a parameter. In those cases, if you don't want the parameters to be linked, you can get rid of the expression by typing a new value in the number field or dragging a slider.

12   Click in the number field for bLo, type in *.25*, and press Enter.

Rendering Your Tree

The final step is to save your script out and render the darn thing.

1   Select the node you want to actually render out, in this case the Over1 node.

You can, however, output as many files as you want. For example, if you were working with film images, you could attach an Image - FileOut to composite your high-resolution files and then also have a video resolution FileOut going straight to a digital disk recorder. You can add as many FileOut nodes as you need to any point in your tree.

2   Select FileOut from the Image tab.

When you click on Image - FileOut, the browser pops up.

3   Go to your Home directory and select the Shake_Output folder that you created.

4   Enter a filename, *my_fish_comp.#.iff*, at the bottom of the File Browser and click OK.

The image filename should contain three things:

▶   The image name.

▶   A symbol for the frame, either # or @, which represents a padded or unpadded placeholder.

▶   An extension: .iff = IFF files, .tif = TIFF files, .tga = TGA files, and so on. There are about 20 different formats, which can be viewed under File Formats.

NOTE ▶ The IFF file format is the native Shake file format.

Therefore, if you enter a name, something like *test.#.iff*, Shake will write out test.0001.iff, test.0002.iff, and so on. If you type *test.@.cin*, your output files will write out as test.1.cin, test.2.cin, test.3.cin, and so on.

5   Resave the tree by choosing File > Save Script.

6   Click on the FileOut node, and select Render > Render FileOut Nodes.

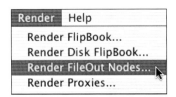

A window will pop up giving you some choices.

7   The default settings are fine, so just click the Render button.

A Monitor window will appear to show you the progress of your render. Unlike a normal flipbook, only the current frame is loaded into memory. Previous frames are discarded from the Monitor window. Additionally, the Monitor window is always the same resolution (360×240), regardless of the output resolution settings. When the render finishes, you can load the frames into a flipbook to see them.

8 When the render is finished, close the Monitor window.

9 Open up a new FileIn node, and if you don't see the file you just rendered, click on the Force Update icon at the top right of the File Browser.

This refreshes the File Browser, and your rendered sequence is now listed.

10 Double-click on the my_fish_comp.1-50#.iff sequence you just rendered.

11 Click the Flipbook icon to load my_fish_comp.

12 Press the > key to play the clip.

Pat yourself on the back; you've created and rendered your first Shake composite.

13 Quit Shake.

What You've Learned

- You can attach nodes in the Node workspace in multiple ways, including clicking a node in the Tool tabs, right-clicking a node in the Tool tabs, and with the Tools menu.

- The standard practice for layering operations that expect two input images is to connect the foreground to the first, or left, input and the background to the second, or right, input.

- You can automatically organize your nodes by deselecting them all and pressing the L key.

- The Over node expects premultiplied images.

- The MDiv (Matte Divide) node undoes premultiplication.

Keyboard Shortcuts

Tool Tabs

Left mouse click	inserts node after selected node
Shift-click	creates new branch off selected node
Ctrl-click	replaces currently selected node
Shift-Ctrl-click	creates unconnected node

Node Workspace

Cmd-X	removes selected nodes and places them into the paste buffer
Cmd-C	copies the selected nodes into the paste buffer
Cmd-V	pastes nodes and text into the Node View
Delete	deletes the selected nodes
Cmd-Z	undoes up to 100 steps
Cmd-Y	redoes your steps unless you have changed values after you have done several undos

Keyboard Shortcuts (continued)

Node Workspace

+	zooms into the Node View
-	zooms out of the Node View
Home	centers all nodes
F	frames all selected nodes into the Node View
O	toggles on the Overview window to help navigate in the Node View
Cmd-F	activates nodes according to what to you enter in the Search string field
Cmd-A	selects all nodes
Shift-A	selects all nodes attached to the current group
Shift-U	selects nodes upstream from the currently active node
Shift-D	selects nodes downstream from the currently active node
Shift-up arrow	adds one upstream node to the current selection
Shift-down arrow	adds one downstream node to the current selection
L	performs an automated layout on the selected nodes
X	snaps all selected nodes into the same column

Keyboard Shortcuts (continued)

Node Workspace

Y

snaps all selected nodes into the same row

G

visually collapses selected nodes into one node; press again to ungroup

M

opens a group into a subwindow

I

turns off selected nodes when activated; select them again and press I to reactivate

E

pulls the active nodes from the tree, reconnecting the remaining nodes to each other

Shift-M

launches the MacroMaker with the selected nodes as the macro body

B

opens up a macro into a subwindow so you can review wiring and parameters

Alt-B

closes up the macro subwindow when the cursor is placed outside of the open macro

Parameters Workspace

Ctrl-drag (while over a parameter value)

changes the value interactively, left-drag to lower the value, right-drag to raise the value

Tab

advances to next text field

Shift-Tab

goes to previous text field

Right-click

accesses to a pop-up menu

Drag a parameter name

copies parameter to target parameter

Shift-drag a parameter name

links parameter from target parameter

3

Lesson Files   Lessons > Lesson03 folder

Media   beach_cu.iff

beach_ws.iff

flowers.iff

hiker.iff

mountains.iff

sunset.iff

Time   approximately 45 minutes

Goals   Manipulate images with Shake's color correction tools

Concatenate color nodes

Use the Color Picker

Color match shots that have differing colors

Lesson 3
Color Correction

Color correction is a generic term for any process that alters the
perceived color of an image. The mere mention of the term sends
shivers up my spine, because no two people can ever agree on
what looks right, including your clients. The perception of color
will no doubt be different for every person who looks at your
monitor. So, charge by the hour and color correction will be your
friend. Fortunately, Shake provides you with a vast array of color
manipulation tools with which to drive up your profits.

The Shake Color tab.

Basic Color Correction Tools

Shake's color is typically described in an RGB range between 0 and 1. The Color nodes are generally either mathematical corrections to color (for example, add .5 to the red channel), or the rearranging of specific color channels.

Many of the color-correction nodes can have identical results. For example, Mult and Brightness are the same command, except Brightness affects all three RGB channels at the same time, whereas Mult allows you to adjust each individual channel. Additionally, other functions such as Lookup and ColorX can also duplicate most of the other color nodes. Although ColorX is the most powerful and complicated node in the Color tab, it is also the slowest because it acts on each individual pixel.

Shake's basic color correctors are split up into atomic nodes that can be rearranged in any fashion you wish. The basic nodes are as follows:

Add

The Add function adds to the R, G, B, or A channels. It will also add color to black areas, including those beyond the image frame, in case you move the image later on.

Brightness

This function is simply a multiplier on the RGB channels and is useful for brightening or darkening an image.

ContrastLum

ContrastLum applies a contrast change on the image, with a smooth falloff on both the low and high ends.

Gamma

A gamma correction affects only the midtones while retaining the black and white values of an image. Pixels with a value of 0 or 1 are unaffected. Only nonblack or nonwhite pixels are adjusted.

Mult

This function multiplies the R, G, B, or A channels. Unlike Add, the Mult operator does not add color to black areas.

Lookup

This performs an arbitrary lookup on your image. It is extremely flexible, allowing you to mimic most other color correction nodes. It's also handy for adjusting color values using a curve.

Reorder

The Reorder operator lets you shuffle channels. The argument to this command specifies the new order. A channel can be copied to several different channels.

Using the Color Nodes

It's time to try out a few of the Color nodes.

1 Start Shake.

2 Select File > Open Script.

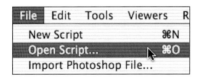

3 Go to the Lesson03/scripts folder and load the **color1.shk** script.

This script has a scenic mountain image connected to some basic color correction nodes.

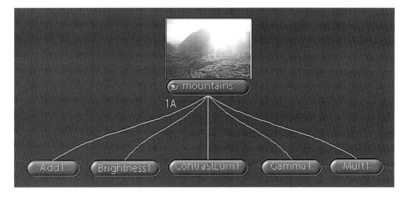

Mountains photo courtesy of Thinkstock images.

4   Double-click on the Add1 node.

You'll see a + next to the Color parameter. This means that extra parameters can be unfolded.

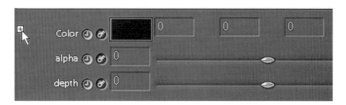

5   Click on the + next to the Color parameter.

This reveals a series of radio buttons with another + to the left of them.

6   Click on the + next to the R radio button.

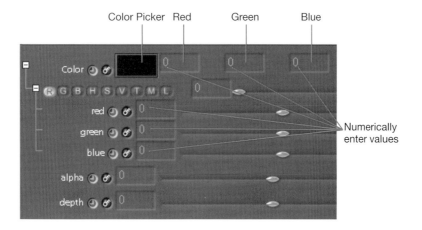

When tuning parameters within the color nodes, you can choose several methods:

▶ Numerically enter values in the RGB text fields.

▶ Drag the slider next to each text field.

▶ Click the Color Picker and select a color from the screen or from the color wheel.

▶ Use the Virtual Color Picker. If you hold the keyboard character R(ed), G(reen), B(lue), H(ue), S(aturation), V(alue), L(uminance), M(agenta), or T(emperature) and drag left and right in the Parameters workspace, you will modify that parameter.

▶ To gang up the red, green, and blue sliders, hold down V (for Value) and drag left and right.

7 Hold down the R key and drag to the right.

This will add to the red channel.

8 Once you have added red, hold down the H key and drag left and right.

This shifts the hue of the color. Modifying using this manner modifies only the color that is added, multiplied, and so on. For example, by dragging a color while pressing S (for saturation) it will not decrease the saturation on the image, only the saturation of the color that you are adding to the image.

9   Now let's view and edit each of the other Color nodes attached to the mountains node by double-clicking on it. Go ahead and experiment by adjusting each node's parameters to see how it affects the image.

When you are done working with the color nodes attached to the mountains image, move onto the tree with the sunset image.

Sunset photo courtesy of Thinkstock Images.

10   Now double-click on the Reorder1 node attached to the sunset node.

The Reorder function allows you to easily move the channels around.

11   To copy the red channel to all three channels, leaving the alpha alone, type *rra* in the channels parameter.

All three color channels come from the red channel.

12   View each color channel ending with the alpha channel in the Viewer by clicking on the View RGBA Channels button.

13 To remove the alpha channel, type *rgbn* in the Channels parameter.

The alpha channel turns black.

14 To copy the luminance into the Matte channel, type *rgbl*.

The letter *l* refers to luminance, which is the average luminance of the color channels.

15 Press the C key in the Viewer to show the RGB channels.

These are just the basic color correction tools in Shake; many more are located in the Color tab.

Using PlotScanline to Understand Color Corrections

To help you better understand some of Shake's color correction functions, a useful operator called PlotScanline is included. It is designed to look at a single horizontal scan-line of an image and plot the brightness of a pixel for each X location. This allows you to graphically see how a color correction node is affecting the image.

1 Select File > New Script.

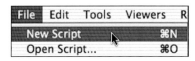

2 Answer No when prompted to save the current script.

3 Click on the Ramp node in the Image tab.

4   Set the width parameter to *256* and the height parameter to *256*.

The ramp is 256 pixels wide and ranges in value from 0 to 1. This provides a 1:1 correspondence between the range of possible values in an 8-bit image.

5   Add the PlotScanline operator from the Other tab after Ramp1.

The PlotScanline curve indicates that this is a linear ramp.

6 Now insert a color correction operator such as ContrastLum from the Color tab into the chain, after Ramp1 and before the PlotScanline1.

7 Set the value parameter to *1.5* and set the softClip parameter to *1.0*.

This will modify the gradient, and the plot will reflect this. As you adjust the values of your contrast, the plot updates to reflect any changes.

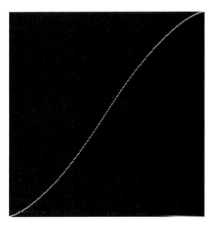

The image is effectively a plot of the Contrast function.

8   View Ramp1, ContrastLum1, and then PlotScanline1 in turn to see
    how the adjustment affects the image.

    PlotScanline is also capable of graphing the different channels of an
    image separately.

9   Replace ContrastLum1 with a Gamma node located in the Color tab.

10 Adjust the rGamma, gGamma, and bGamma parameters to be differ-
    ent values.

    There are now three curves representing red, green, and blue values.

11 Place different color nodes in place of Gamma1 and see how
    PlotScanline reacts as the various parameters are adjusted.

Concatenation

A unique aspect of Shake's color handling is that it concatenates color
corrections. This means that if you have 10 Color operations in a row,
Shake will mathematically compile them into 1 operation. You don't have
to spend the time processing the 10 nodes, just 1. An important second
benefit is that if you darken an image by half and then double its brightness, the adjustments cancel each other out, leaving no change. Without

this functionality, you would be throwing data away when you darken the image and you will not be able to recover it by brightening it in a second operation.

The following functions concatenate together:

- Add
- Brightness
- Clamp
- Color Match
- Compress
- ContrastRGB (but not ContrastLum)
- DelogC
- Expand
- Fade
- Gamma
- Invert
- LogC
- Lookup
- Mult
- Set
- Solarize

Furthermore, AdjustHSV and LookupHSV concatenate only with each other. If you have a hard time remembering which nodes concatenate with each other, you can tell by the C in the top-left corner of a node. If it has a C, it concatenates with other nodes that show a C.

NOTE ▶ Concatenation occurs only on adjacent nodes. If you attach a different class of node between two nodes that concatenate with each other, it will break the concatenation.

Color Matching Using Channel Isolation

Very often, you will have two images from the same location that are not color matched. By looking at the individual color channels in the Viewer, you can easily color match these types of shots. Once again, I've done most of the setup work for you with the **color2.shk** script.

1   Choose File > Open Script and click No when prompted to save the current script.

2   Select the `color2.shk` script from the Lesson03/scripts folder.

You'll see a composite of a lifeguard tower in the center of a beach with a definite mismatch in color. Take a look at the elements.

3   View the `beach_ws` and `beach_cu` clips.

These are two shots of the beach with different framing and color correction. Now, take a look at the components of the composite.

4   View each node of the tree starting with RotoShape1 and ending with Over1.

The `beach_cu` clip has a RotoShape to cut it out and a Move2D to match the size and position to the `beach_ws` clip. The modified `beach_cu` is then placed on top of `beach_ws` with an Over. To fix this color mismatch, you can use a Mult function.

5   Insert a Mult node between Move2D1 and Over1.

6   Expand the Color channels by first clicking on the + next to the Color parameter and then the + next to the R button.

7   In the Viewer, look only at the red channel. By isolating individual color channels, it is easier to match the colors.

8   Adjust the red slider until the lifeguard cutout matches the background.

You may find it difficult to match the two images exactly using the slider. You can adjust the red parameter with more accuracy by using the virtual sliders, which change the value interactively and give you finer control—left-drag lowers the value, right-drag raises the value. The virtual sliders are activated when you Ctrl-drag in the red parameter box.

9   Adjust the red virtual slider.

TIP ▶ Set your Update mode to Always. As you drag a parameter, Shake is constantly rendering. This makes the color adjustments more interactive.

10   In the Viewer, look only at the green channel.

11   Adjust the green parameter by using the virtual sliders.

12 In the Viewer, look only at the blue channel.

13 Adjust the blue parameter until the lifeguard cutout matches the background.

14 Now look at the RGB channels in the Viewer at the same time.

The lifeguard tower is now perfectly matched (depending on your standards) to the background. Another way to color match the two shots would be with the ColorMatch node, explained in the following section.

Color Matching Using ColorMatch

ColorMatch allows you to apply a color correction to an image by taking an old set of colors (source color) and matching them up to a new set (destination color) by adjusting the low, middle, and high values of the image. You can also do Contrast, Gamma, Mult, and Add color corrections.

When you match color and use the Color Picker, a good workflow is to first select all three source colors and then select the destination colors. Otherwise, you may pick colors that have been modified.

> **TIP** ▶ Another technique to use when scrubbing is to ignore the node while scrubbing (select the node and press I in the Node View) and then turn it on when finished.

Let's try to match the beach shots by using the ColorMatch node.

1 Extract the Mult1 node by highlighting it and pressing the E key.

   This automatically extracts the node from the tree.

2 Place a ColorMatch node after **beach_ws**.

3 Double-click on ColorMatch1 to make it the active node.

   You'll start by selecting the low, mid, and high source colors.

4 Click on the Color Picker tab in the Node workspace.

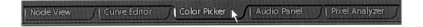

The Color Picker, which is in a tab on the Node workspace by default, allows the sampling of values from the Viewer, which can then be dragged and dropped to other parameters. It includes handy analysis tools for finding and comparing different color values on your image. You can examine minimum, average, current, or maximum pixel values, which are particularly useful, naturally, when doing color corrections.

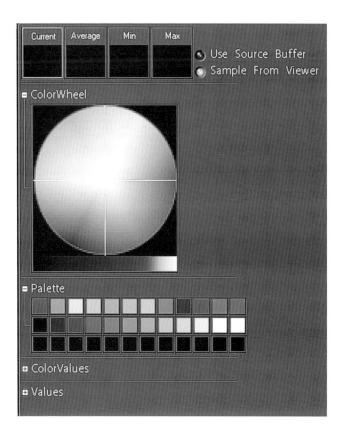

5   Drag across the image.

As you drag across the image, the values will show up in the Color Picker constantly updating the Min, Max, Average, and Current color boxes.

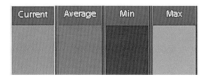

In matching the two beach shots, the first step is to choose the shadows, or darkest areas of the screen.

6   Zoom into the guy sitting below the lifeguard tower and press the + key repeatedly until you've zoomed in far enough.

7 Drag the cursor over the dark areas of the man's pants.

8 Use the Home key to reset the Viewer's zoom to a 1:1 ratio.

You've sampled a color—now what? Enter ColorMatch1's lowSource Color values using drag and drop.

9 To do this, click once on the Current color box so that it is selected.

10 Click and hold on the Current color box in the Color Picker and drag and drop onto the Color Picker next to lowSource in ColorMatch1.

Now you can set the midSource and highSource values.

11 Click on the midSource Color Picker.

When you click directly on a Color Picker within a node's parameters, the Color Picker will automatically open. Once you pick a color from the Viewer, it will automatically be entered as a parameter value.

12 Select the midSource color according to the following picture:

High source   Low source   Mid source

13 Click on the highSource Color Picker and select the highSource color according to the preceding picture.

Now that the source colors are selected, you can select the destination colors.

14 Change the Node workspace from the Color Picker to the Node View.

15 Click on the left side of the `beach_cu` node so that you can sample colors from that shot.

16 Select the low, mid, and high destination colors from this shot.

High destination   Mid destination

Low destination

17 Change the Node workspace from the Color Picker to the Node View.

18 Click on the left side of the Over1 node so that you can view it.

Close, but no cigar. You'll need to do a little adjustment by hand.

19 Look at the individual R, G, and B channels in the Viewer and adjust the midDest Red, Green, and Blue values by using the channel isolation technique from the last exercise.

The ColorCorrect Node

ColorCorrect combines Add, Mult, Gamma, ContrastRGB, ColorReplace, Invert, Reorder, and Lookup all into one node, giving you the ability to tune the image in only the shadow, midtone, or highlight areas. ColorCorrect will also give your clients all of the needed controls to endlessly noodle with your shots. Not to worry, you are charging by the hour, remember?

> **NOTE** ▶ ColorCorrect will break concatenation with connecting color corrections.

1 Select File > New Script and answer No when prompted to save your script.

2 FileIn the **hiker.iff** clip from the Lesson03 folder.

3 Attach a ColorCorrect node from the Color tab.

Color Correct Subtabs

The ColorCorrect node is organized into the following seven subtabs:

Subtab	Description
Master	applies the correction to the entire image
Low Controls	applies the correction primarily to the darkest portion of the image, with the correction falling off as the image gets brighter
Mid Controls	applies the correction primarily to the middle range of the image
High Controls	applies the correction primarily to the highlights of the image, with falloff as the image gets darker
Curves	applies manual correction to the image using curves
Misc	performs secondary color correction, as well as invert, reorder, and premultiplication control
Range Curves	displays the different image ranges (shadows, midtones, highlights), their control curves, and the final concatenated curve of the color correction

The Master, Low, Mid, and High Controls Tabs

The first four tabs are identical except for the portion of the image that they allow you to modify. Each has controls to Add, multiply (Gain), and apply a Gamma to the RGB channels, as well as apply contrast on a per-channel basis (Contrast, Center, and SoftClip).

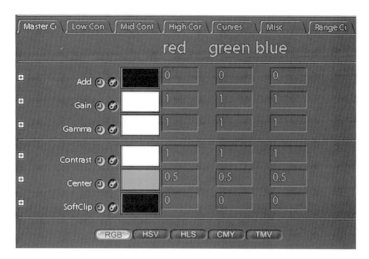

At the bottom of the tab is a display toggle to switch the channels from RGB display to a different color space model. You can modify it to display RGB, HSV, HLS, CMY, or TMV (Temperature/Magenta-Cyan/Value).

1   Click on the button at the bottom marked HSV.

The numbers are converted to HSV space.

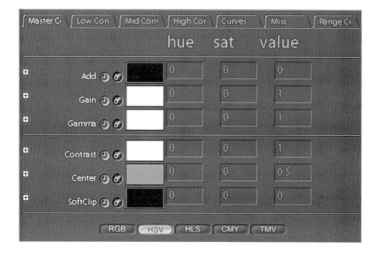

2 Switch back to RGB mode by clicking on the RGB button.

Each Color Picker has an AutoKey and View Curves button associated with all three channels for that parameter. All three channels are treated equally.

NOTE ▶ When ColorCorrect is saved into a script, the values are always stored in RGB space.

Working with Low/Mid/High Ranges

Here is the difference when working with Low, Mid, and High. This is the original image:

1 Click on the Mid Controls tab in the ColorCorrect1 node.

2 Adjust the Blue Gain to *1.5*.

Blue is only added to the midtones of the image, which are the areas of the sky and snow.

3 Select the High Controls tab.

4 Adjust the Blue Gain to a value of *.75*.

Only the highlights of this image are adjusted, which makes the clouds a warm yellow color. You can also control the range of the image's shadows, midtones, and highlights by going to the Range Curves tab.

5 Select the Range Curves tab.

This tab displays your final color correction, as well as the Low, Mid, and High mask ranges, as curves. You can also use the display toggle to switch the output from the normal, corrected image to a display of the Low areas, the Mid areas, or the High areas. A colored display was used rather than one based on luminance since different channels will have different values.

6 Click on the ViewL, ViewM, and ViewH buttons.

ViewL   ViewM   ViewH

7 To control the mask areas, turn off the Color display and turn on the Ranges display at the bottom of the Range Curves tab.

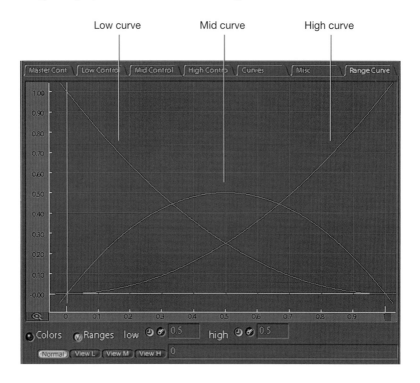

Here are the curves for the low, mid, and high values. These curves can be modified by adjusting the low and high parameters.

8 Right-click on the Parameters workspace and select Reset All Values.

Curves Tab

The Curves tab allows you to apply manual modifications to the lookup curve by mapping input colors to output colors.

1 Click on the Curves tab.

2   Turn on the bExpr radio button on the right side of the parameter.

3   Insert some new knots (or points) by Shift-clicking on a segment of
the curve and dragging the newly created points to correct the image.

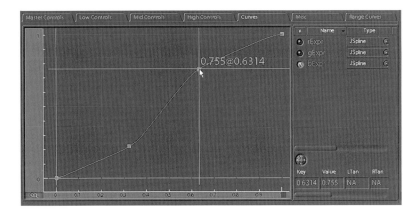

Color correcting using curves can yield results that are hard to duplicate with any other method.

Misc Tab

1   Select File > New Script and answer No when prompted to save
your script.

2   FileIn the **flowers.iff** clip from the Lesson03 folder.

3   Attach the **flowers.iff** clip to a ColorCorrect node.

4   Click on the Misc tab.

This Misc tab has several functions in it:

▶ Invert—Inverts the red, green, and blue channels.

▶ reorderChannels—By entering a string, you can swap or remove your channels as per the standard Reorder method.

▶ preMultiplied—Toggle this on if your image is premultiplied (typically, an image coming from a computer-generated render), and it will automatically insert an MDiv before the calculations and an MMult afterwards.

▶ Color Replace—This is the same as the ColorReplace node located in the Color tab. It allows you to isolate a color according to its hue, saturation, and value, and replace it with a different color. Other areas of the spectrum will remain unchanged. This is especially handy for spill suppression when performing keying operations.

NOTE ▶ There is a toggle to affect the alpha channel in the stand-alone ColorReplace node in case you also want to pull a mask of the affected source color.

Next, you will isolate the red flowers and change their color.

5   Click on the Source Color Picker.

6 Select one of the red flowers in the Viewer.

7 Now click on the Destination Color Picker and drag the Color Picker to a blue color.

The flowers have only partially turned blue. If you adjust some of the Range/Falloff parameters, you can get it just right.

8   Adjust the hueRange to a value of *0* and satRange to a value of *.5*.

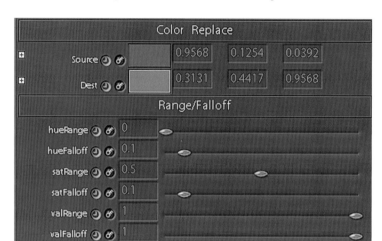

The flowers should now look completely blue.

9   Quit Shake.

What You've Learned

- The PlotScanline tool provides a visual representation of a color operation.

- Concatenation is very useful because you can perform numerous Color operations as a single operation.

- The Color Picker allows you to select colors.

- The ColorReplace function enables you to replace one color with another.

Keyboard Shortcuts

Virtual Color Picker	works with any color swatch or numerical entry area involving color values
R-drag	adjusts Red
G-drag	adjusts Green
B-drag	adjusts Blue
H-drag	adjusts Hue
S-drag	adjusts Saturation
V-drag	adjusts Value
L-drag	adjusts Luminance
C-drag	adjusts Cyan
M-drag	adjusts Magenta
Y-drag	adjusts Yellow
T-drag	adjusts Temperature

4

Lesson Files	Lessons > Lesson04 folder
Media	bathroom.1-46.iff
	blob.1-46.iff
	blob_comp.1-46.iff
Time	approximately 30 minutes
Goals	Composite two clips
	Manipulate images with the On-Screen controls
	Make mattes with the RotoShape node

Intermediate Compositing, Part 1

In this lesson, you will delve farther into the depths of Shake's compositing features. The lesson covers key concepts such as compositing modes and drawing shapes.

In this lesson you will create this composite from two different clips.

Essentials of Compositing

The visual effects supervisor has just dumped a shot on you. It consists of two elements. How do you put them together? As always, it depends. There is never really a right way. Here's my way.

Loading Images

1   Start Shake.

2   Select FileIn from the Image tab and go to the Lesson04 folder.

3   FileIn all the clips in this folder by pressing Cmd-A and clicking OK.

    The **bathroom**, **blob**, and **blob_comp** clips all appear in the Node workspace.

4   Set the Globals timeRange by clicking the Auto button.

    The Globals timeRange is automatically set to the length of the longest clip.

5   Double-click on the **blob_comp** clip, click the Flipbook icon and play the clip.

    This is what your final composite will look like. As you can see, a squishy, blob-shaped creature is tip-toeing across the screen.

6   Make flipbooks of the **blob** and **bathroom** clips and play them.

These are the elements to be used in your composite.

7   Close all your flipbooks and then double-click the **blob** clip to select and view it.

8   Go to frame 23 by dragging the Time Bar.

The **blob** clip has an alpha channel that will be used to layer it over the **bathroom** clip.

9   With the cursor in the Viewer window, press the A key to look at the **blob** clip's alpha channel. Press the C key when done to view the clip in color.

Both of the elements are 46 frames long, so you're going to set the Time Bar to 46 frames. Since the Globals timeRange has already been set to 1-46, you can automatically set the Time Bar to the same value by clicking on the Home icon.

10 Click on the Home icon at the bottom-right corner of the interface.

The Time Bar is automatically set to the Globals timeRange.

Thumbnails

If you look at the Node workspace, you might notice the pretty thumbnails. Each of these is a function that you can look at and modify. It just so happens that these are all FileIn functions that read in images.

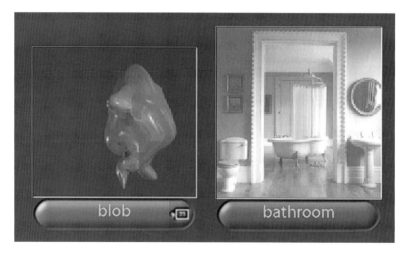

As you can see from the blob image in the preceding example, the thumbnails also indicate transparency if there is an accompanying alpha channel.

A bit about the thumbnails:

- They take frame 1 as the thumbnail by default.
- To refresh to the current frame, select the node and press R in the Node View.

- To see the alpha channel, place the cursor over the thumbnail and press A. To return to RGB color, press C with the cursor over the thumbnail.

- Any node can have a thumbnail—just select it and press R.

- To hide thumbnails, select the ones you want to hide and press T. Press T again to see the thumbnails.

- Under the Globals tab, reveal the guiSettings and you can change the displayThumbnails control. This is the same as pressing T in the Node view.

Here's a nifty trick: Drag the blob node over the bathroom node in the Node workspace.

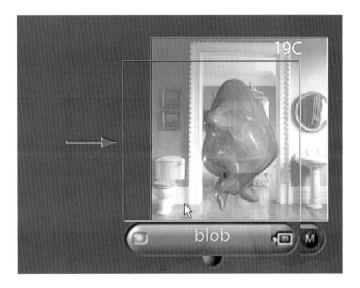

Shake does a mini composite for you. Does this help you composite or change your tree at all? Nope, but it's cool, isn't it? To do an actual composite, you have to hook up the nodes. You will do that soon, so stop fidgeting.

Setting Resolution

Shake makes it easy to composite images of different resolutions.

1 With the **blob** clip highlighted, select Layer from the Layer tab.

The Layer node automatically connects itself to the **blob** clip and incorporates most of the other Layer operations, with the exception of KeyMix and AddText. There is no particular advantage to using Layer instead of one of the specific layer operations, except that you can try out different modes quickly.

2 Connect the **bathroom** clip to the right input of the Layer1 node.

The default compositing operation in the Layer node is an Over function that places the foreground over the background based on the foreground clip's alpha channel. This is what you want.

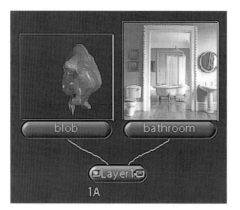

You may have observed that the **blob** image is a smaller resolution (201 × 175 pixels) than the **bathroom** image (388 × 388 pixels) and that the resolution of the composite is cropped to the smaller size of the **blob** clip. The resolution is printed either in the Viewer title bar, or in the help field at the bottom of the screen when hovering over a clip.

Shake allows you to composite images of different resolutions through the use of the clipMode parameter contained in every Layer node. In this case, the Layer node defaults to the resolution of the foreground clip.

3   Toggle the clipMode back and forth to select the foreground or the background as your output resolution. When you're done, leave the clipMode set to background.

4   Drag the Time Bar back and forth so that you can see the blob moving across the screen.

Before you get too far into this composite, you should save your script.

5   Choose File > Save Script.

The browser will appear and wait for you to type in a name.

6   Open your Home directory and select the Shake_Output folder that you created in Lesson 2.

7   In the File name path, type the name of your script and click OK.

TIP ▶ Get in the habit of saving your scripts periodically as you add new elements, because who knows when your cat will finally chew through your computer cables and leave you without power.

Transforming Images

Did you see that the blob gets cut off at frame 1 and should be repositioned? You can use the Move2D node to transform or move the image.

1 Insert a Move2D node from the Transform tab between the **blob** clip and the Layer1 node. To do this, first select **blob** and then click on Move2D.

The Move2D function combines many of the other transform nodes together, including Pan, Scale, Shear, and Rotate.

When the parameters for Move2D1 come up, Shake conveniently pops up some On-Screen controls in the Viewer to help you.

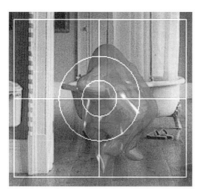

The button that turns on the On-Screen controls is located under the Viewer and has three positions.

2   Click and hold on the On-Screen controls icon to bring up the
pop-up list.

▶   This means the controls are always on. This is the mode you want
to be in to interactively drag an image around.

▶   The controls disappear if you move the image. They reappear
when you release the mouse.

▶   The controls are always off, but you can still move the image in
the Viewer by using the sliders in the Parameters workspace.

The On-Screen controls work like this:

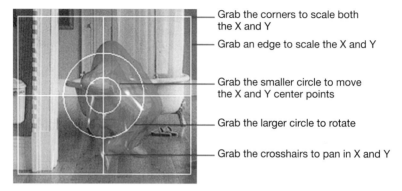

Grab the corners to scale both the X and Y

Grab an edge to scale the X and Y

Grab the smaller circle to move the X and Y center points

Grab the larger circle to rotate

Grab the crosshairs to pan in X and Y

If you don't like the colors of the On-Screen controls, you can change them with the On-Screen controls Color Picker.

3 Click on the On-Screen controls Color Picker and it brings up the Color Picker in the Node workspace.

4 In the Palette, click on the red color square.

The On-Screen controls turn red.

5   Click on the white square to turn the On-Screen controls back to white.

Now that you know how to turn the On-Screen controls on and off and change their colors, you can be trusted to use the Move2D node.

6   Click on the Node View tab under the Node workspace to remove the Color Picker and see your nodes.

7   Drag the **blob** clip around with the various On-Screen controls.

When you use the On-Screen controls, you are automatically entering values for the xPan, yPan, angle, xScale, and yScale parameters in the Move2D node. You can also adjust these parameters by moving the sliders.

TIP ▶ A cool trick is to use Ctrl-drag in the numeric text field on the slider—this gives you virtual sliders that go beyond the range of the graphic sliders.

Before you proceed, you should reset the node. This will bring all of the parameters back to their default settings.

8   Reset the Move2D1 parameters by right-clicking in the Parameters1 window and selecting Reset All Values.

9   At frame 1, use the On-Screen controls to place the right edge of the blob on the right side of the doorway. If you want to type in the exact values, they are xPan=73 and yPan=41.

10 Drag the Time Bar back and forth.

The blob moves across the screen, but is always in front of the bathroom door. This is pretty obvious when you get to frame 46 or so. What you really want is to place the blob inside the bathroom. To do this, you'll have to draw a matte for the opening of the door.

Creating RotoShapes

The RotoShape function is an image generator that is used for animated garbage mattes. This is where you draw shapes that can be used for a variety of purposes. It is ideal for plugging into the Mask input of a node, or to be used in conjunction with functions such as Inside, Outside, or KeyMix. More on this in a moment.

Since RotoShape creates images like any other node, you can modify them with standard tools such as Blur or DilateErode.

1   Click on the RotoShape node from the Image tab.

   A RotoShape node is created in the Node workspace.

2   Make sure the On-Screen controls are in the always visible position.

3   Click on the left side of the **bathroom** clip to view it.

   You should now see the **bathroom** clip with RotoShape1's On-Screen controls overlaid on it.

4   Make sure the AutoKey button located under the Viewer is in the off position.

   When on, the Viewer AutoKey button will set keyframes every time the shape or its knots (or points) are moved. The shape will not be animated, so it's best to leave the AutoKey button off here.

   ▶   AutoKey off

   ▶   AutoKey on

   By default, the RotoShape node sets itself to video resolution (720×486), so you'll want to change the resolution to be the same size as the **bathroom** clip.

5   Set the width and height parameters to *388*.

RotoShape starts in Add Shapes mode, which means that every time you click on a blank spot, you append a new knot or point between the last knot and the first knot.

6   Click on each corner of the inside of the door to add knots on the screen and close the shape by clicking on the first knot you added.

As soon as the shape is closed, the RotoShape node automatically goes into Edit Shapes mode, where you can adjust the knots.

7   Click on the left side of the RotoShape1 node to view it.

Once the shape is closed, it is filled with a solid white color.

8   Click the left side of the bathroom node so that you can see what you are doing when you modify the shape.

9   Adjust the knots at the bottom corners of the door by clicking and dragging them so that they extend to the bottom of the screen.

10   Highlight the Rotoshape1 node and press the R key to generate a thumbnail.

A thumbnail for the RotoShape appears. It's magic.

Compositing Functions

Now that you've drawn a shape, there are various ways to use it in your composite to place the blob inside the bathroom. To start with, you'll need to integrate RotoShape1 with the **bathroom** clip, and since you're already familiar with an Over composite, you'll try an Atop composite in conjunction with a Copy node.

1   Go to frame 43 of the composite.

2   Add a Copy node from the Layer tab after the **bathroom** clip.

The Copy function copies selected channels from image B to image A, replacing them entirely. You commonly copy over the alpha channel.

3   Connect the RotoShape1 node to the right input of Copy1.

4   Double-click on the Copy1 node to view and edit it.

5   In the Channels parameter of the Copy1 node, type an *A*.

This will place the Alpha channel of RotoShape1 into the **bathroom** clip. Take a quick look.

6   Toggle the Viewer to show the alpha channel and then toggle it back to show full color.

7   Double-click on the Layer1 node and then click on the operation pop-up menu.

8   Select Atop from the operation menu.

Atop is similar to Over, except that the background matte is also used; the foreground will appear only where there is background matte.

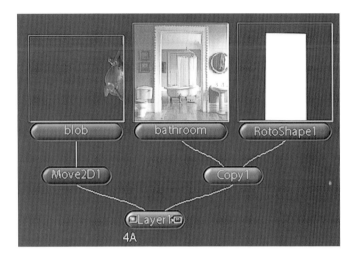

Mr. Blob is now behind the door.

As always, there are a number of different ways to accomplish the same result. Let's try another approach.

9 Switch Layer1's operation mode back to Over.

10 Insert an Inside node from the Layer tab between Move2D1 and the Layer1 node.

The Inside node places one image inside the mask of a second image. Only the second image's mask is considered in the composite, the rest comes from the color of the foreground image.

11 Connect the output of the RotoShape1 node to the right input of the Inside1 node.

You don't need the Copy1 node anymore, so go ahead and delete it.

12 Remove the Copy1 node by clicking on it and pressing Del.

The Copy1 node is deleted, and the noodle keeps the **bathroom** clip connected to the Layer1 node.

Your tree should look like this:

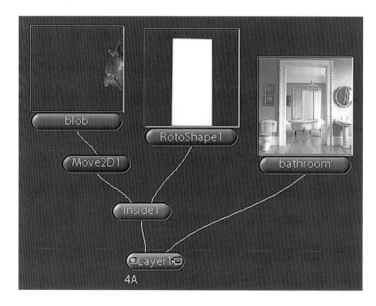

13 Double-click on the Layer1 node and scroll through the composite.

The blob is behind the door and the composite looks good, so it's time to make a flipbook.

14 Click the Flipbook icon.

15 Play the clip with the > key.

Looks pretty good, but something's not quite right. There's no drop shadow. Every respectable blob creates a drop shadow, doesn't it? In Lesson 5, you will continue this tutorial by adding a drop shadow as well as some other goodies to make the blob really fit into the scene.

16 Select File > Save Script.

In the next lesson, you will load this script you continue where you left off.

17 Quit Shake.

What You've Learned

*   Any node can have a thumbnail—just select it and press R.

*   The RotoShape node is used to create shapes.

*   Atop is similar to Over, except that the background matte is also used in the composite; the foreground will appear only where there is a background matte.

*   The Copy function copies selected channels from image B to image A.

*   The Inside node places one image inside the mask of a second image.

Keyboard Shortcuts

Thumbnails

R	refreshes thumbnail at the current frame
T	hides/shows thumbnails
A	shows the alpha channel of thumbnail
C	thumbnail in full color

5

Lesson Files	Lessons > Lesson05 folder
Media	blob_pt1.shk
Time	approximately 30 minutes
Goals	Make a drop shadow using a mask
	Create and edit keyframes to animate over time
	Add realistic refractions and match film grain

Lesson **5**

Intermediate Compositing, Part 2

Normally you can get 95 percent of a shot done very quickly. It's always that last 5 percent that takes the majority of the time and effort but makes the difference in whether or not the shot looks real. In this lesson, which continues the blob composite, you will use keyframing to animate parameters as well as use masks to limit the effect of filters.

You can see the motion path in Shake as you set keyframes.

Creating a Drop Shadow

To make the blob from the last lesson really fit into the scene, it needs a drop shadow. You will make one by using a Brightness node that will be limited to the area of the blob's mask.

1   Start Shake.

2   Choose File > Open Script.

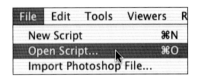

3   Navigate to the Lesson05/scripts folder and choose **blob_pt1.shk**, or select the script that you saved from the previous lesson and click OK.

Your script opens up in the Node workspace.

4   Park the Time Bar at frame 18.

This is a good frame to add the shadow.

5   Insert a Brightness node from the Color tab between the **bathroom** clip and the Layer1 node.

6   Drag a noodle from the output of the Inside1 node to the right side of the Brightness1 node.

An M appears on the side of the node. This is the Mask input.

7   In the Brightness1 node, click on the + to the left of the Mask control
    to expand the Mask parameters.

You can apply a mask to any operation by dragging the output of a
node to the right side of a second node. That node will only process
within the white areas of the channel you specify. When a node has a
mask applied to it, new parameters will appear in the Parameters
workspace, letting you activate the mask, invert the mask, and control
the mask's strength.

The other way to apply a mask to a node is through the Mask Create
function. When you click on the RotoShape pull-down menu next to
Mask:Create, you have six mask creation options that will automatically create a node and connect it to the Mask input of the node you
are editing.

8   Look at the Alpha channel in the Viewer.

    The Brightness1 node will use this mask when creating the drop
    shadow.

9 While viewing the Layer1 node, look at the RGB channels in the Viewer and turn the value parameter in the Brightness1 node to a value of 0.

Only the area behind the blob darkens because you haven't positioned the shadow yet.

10 Insert a Move2D between Inside1 and Brightness1 by selecting the Inside1 node and then clicking the Move2D tool from the Transform tab. You will notice that the Move2D2 node is connected with both the Brightness1 and Layer1 nodes. To bypass the Move2D2 node connection to Layer1, click and drag from the output of the Inside1 node to the left input of the Layer1 node.

11 View the Layer1 node and edit the Move2D2 node.

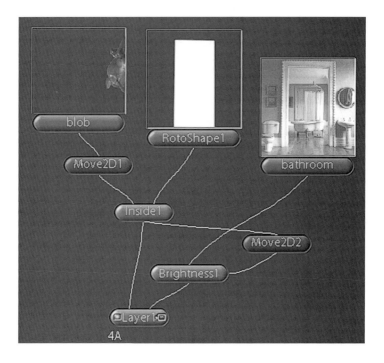

12 Use the On-Screen controls to move the shadow down a bit so that you can see it.

The shadow is really dark right now, but it's best to leave it this way while you are positioning it. Afterwards, you can lighten up the shadow.

13 Set the xScale to 1.2 and yScale to .10.

14 Use the On-Screen controls to place the shadow under the blob's feet. Use the horizontal crosshair or the sliders in the Move2D2 node to do this.

15 Turn off the On-Screen controls for a moment to get a better look at the shadow.

The shadow needs just a wee bit of softness.

16 Insert a Blur node from the Filter tab between the Move2D2 node and the Brightness1 node.

17 Set the xPixels value to about 35.

Did you notice that the yPixels value was automatically set? Shake is always making life easier for you.

18 Drag the Time Bar to view the composite and end on frame 31.

Two problems have reared their ugly heads. The first is the shadow's position. Its placement should animate over time. Second, the shadow appears over the door frame at the end of the composite, and it should be placed inside the mask of the door. You can fix the shadow over the door by using another Inside node.

19 Place an Inside node between the Blur1 node and the Mask input of the Brightness1 node.

20 Connect another output of the RotoShape1 node to the right input of the Inside2 node.

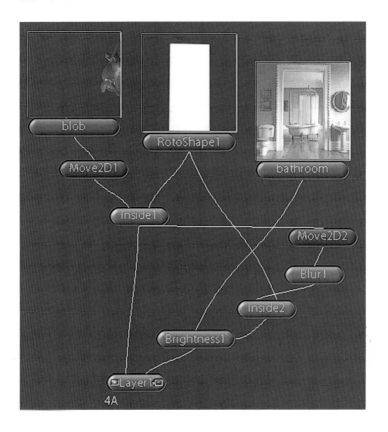

The shadow now appears only within the bathroom door.

21 Double-click on the Layer1 node and drag the Time Bar to view what you've done so far.

Animation

To fix the position of the shadow, you need to animate it over time. Animation is the process of setting values at various frames, or keyframes as they are called. These keyframes transition from one to another over time.

1 Move the Time Bar to frame 1 and click on the right side of Move2D2 to edit its parameters.

2 Turn the On-Screen controls to the position where they disappear when moving, but reappear when you release the mouse.

3 Click the AutoKey button under the Viewer to turn it on.

By turning on the Viewer AutoKey button, you can enter keyframes using the On-Screen controls. The AutoKey button under the Viewer is available for any node that has On-Screen controls.

4 Position the shadow to your liking with the On-Screen controls.

5 Go to frame 29 and position the shadow.

6 Drag the Time Bar between 1 and 29.

When you drag the Time Bar between 1 and 29, you can see little notches in the Time Bar where you have set keyframes.

If you position the Time Bar over one of the notches, you can delete that keyframe by clicking the Delete Keyframe icon on the Viewer.

7 Place the Time Bar at frame 29 and click the Delete Keyframe button on the Viewer.

The keyframe at frame 29 is deleted. As my mom used to say, what is wrong with you? You need that keyframe. Let's bring it back.

8 Click the Undo button to get keyframe 29 back.

If you turn off the AutoKey button and reposition the shadow, your changes will be ignored as soon as you move to a different frame.

You can also add keys to a specific parameter by going to that parameter's slider and turning on its specific AutoKey button.

NOTE ▶ When the Viewer AutoKey icon is activated and you're using the On-Screen controls, keyframes are set for all parameters. This is true even if you adjusted only one parameter, such as rotation. Turning on the AutoKey button next to a particular parameter will set keyframes for that parameter only.

9 Turn on the AutoKey buttons next to the xPan and yPan parameters.

Whenever you enter a value either with the sliders or the virtual sliders, that value will be entered as a keyframe.

NOTE ▶ You can't set keyframes with the parameter sliders by turning on the AutoKey button under the Viewer. To set keyframes with the sliders, you must turn on the AutoKey button next to the parameter.

10 Go to frame 11 and use the virtual sliders (Ctrl-drag) in the xPan and yPan parameters to position the shadow.

TIP ▶ If you want to enter a key but don't want to leave the AutoKey on, simply double-click on the AutoKey button when it is off and a keyframe will be entered.

You may have noticed that a motion path has been drawn on the screen as you have been setting keyframes. If you can't see the motion path, move your cursor over the Viewer area.

The display of the motion path is controlled by the Point display pop-up.

11 Click and hold on the Point icon to bring up the pop-up list.

▶ Display motion path spline + keys

▶ Display motion path keys only

▶ Display neither motion path nor keys

You can grab and drag points within the motion path and modify them. When you hover over or grab a point, the XY coordinate is displayed along with the frame number. You may need to zoom in on the points of the motion path to see this information.

12 Go to frames 24, 29, 36, and 46 and set keyframes for the shadow. If you had difficulty in positioning the shadow to match, use the following table to see the keyframes that we used for the completed shot:

Frame	XPan	YPan
1	−28.6	−138.3
11	−45.1	−129.7
24	−33.7	−141.8
29	−45.5	−141.8
36	−9.7	−138.6
46	−24.9	−134.6

13 Navigate to the new keyframes that have been set using the step for-wards/
backwards keyframe buttons at the bottom right of the screen.

Now that the animation of the shadow is complete, set the Brightness of the drop shadow so that it is more subtle.

14 Click on the right side of the Brightness1 parameter and adjust the value parameter to a value of .6.

15 Drag the Time Bar to see what you've done so far.

Not bad, but you can make it even better.

Image Warping and Grain

The blob composite is almost finished. It just needs a few finishing touches. It looks pretty good, but it would look better if the blob had some displace-ment so that the bathroom looked as if it were refracting through the blob. It just so happens that Shake has an IDisplace node that can do this for you. IDisplace warps an image based on a second image's intensity.

Displacement

1 Park the Time Bar at frame 20.

2 Insert an IDisplace node from the Warp tab between Brightness1 and the Layer1 node.

3 Connect an output of the Inside1 node to the right input of the IDisplace1 node.

4   Double-click on the IDisplace to view and edit it at the same time.

The xScale and yScale parameters control the amount of pixels that the image is offset by the second image.

5   Type in *-23* for xScale and *18* for yScale.

A nice displacement effect is being created, but if you really want to make it look better, you'll need to choose a different channel to create the displacement. The xChannel and yChannel parameters determine which channel from the second image is used to distort the first image.

6   For the xChannel parameter, select G for the green channel. Do the same for yChannel.

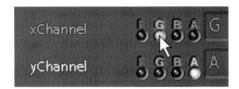

You are now using the green channel from the second image to create the distortion.

Looking at the different channels that are being used to distort the image would be helpful. From the Parameters workspace, you can change what is seen in the Viewer by clicking on the small monitor icon by the name of the input node. You will then load that node into the current Viewer.

7   Click on the small monitor icon next to Background.

This will allow you to view the Inside1 node, which is being used to create the displacement.

8   Place your cursor in the Viewer and toggle through the channels with the R, G, B, and A keys. Finish with the C key to view the RGB channels.

In contrast to the alpha channel, the green channel has more gray tones, which results in a smoother displacement effect.

9   Click on the small monitor icon next to nodeName to view the IDisplace1 node by itself.

NOTE ▶ If you double-click on one of the small monitor icons in the Parameters workspace, you also load that node's parameters.

10   Scroll through the animation with the Time Bar.

This looks pretty good, but what happens when you view the composite through the Layer1 node?

11   Double-click on the Layer1 node and scroll through the animation with the Time Bar again.

When you view the Layer1 node, you can see that much of the displacement effect has been lost. It would help to mix some of the blob out and reveal more of the displacement. You can do this with the Mix node. Mix blends two images together according to a percentage.

12 Insert a Mix function from the Layer tab after Layer1 and connect the output of the IDisplace1 node to the right input of the Mix1 node.

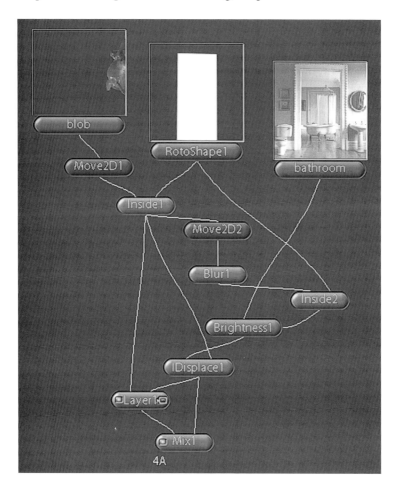

13 Set the percent parameter to 20.

14 Scroll through the animation with the Time Bar.

You're almost done.

Film Grain

To finish off the composite, the blob needs to have grain added so that it matches the grain of the **bathroom** clip. The FilmGrain node is used to simulate film grain and is especially useful to add grain to computer-generated elements. You may apply grain from a preset film stock, match grain to an existing plate, or set your own grain by adjusting sliders. In this exercise, you will match the grain of the **bathroom** clip to the blob.

1   Place a FilmGrain node from the Filter tab after Mix1.

The grain is everywhere, but you want it to appear only on the blob. The FilmGrain's Mask input can take care of this.

2   Take an output of the Inside1 node and connect it to the Mask input of the FilmGrain1 node.

The grain becomes limited to the area within the blob mask. The next step is to place a sample box in an area of the bathroom from which you want to sample grain. The area should be very flat without detail that may disrupt the grain analysis. Small elements will be perceived as grain detail, so your best area in the **bathroom** clip would be the wall on the upper left.

3   Click on the upper-left wall of the **bathroom** clip.

You can drag as many boxes as you want, but for this exercise, you are drawing only one.

NOTE ▶ If you want to remove the grain sample box, click the Undo Last Region icon (below left). Click the Reset the Regions icon (below right) to remove all boxes and start over.

4   Now that you have the grain sample box in place, click the Analyze the Grain icon on the Viewer.

This sets the parameters in the FilmGrain node to match the grain of the **bathroom** clip—well, it's almost a match. It needs one last adjustment to really make it match.

5   Adjust the amount parameter to a value of .5.

Okay, now the grain matches. For those of you interested in minutia, the FilmGrain node has the following parameters:

Parameter	Function
amount	sets the intensity of the grain
size	sets the size of the grain
aspectRatio	sets the aspect ratio of the grain to compensate for anamorphic or nonsquare pixel distortion
seed	sets the random seed for the grain
filmStock	allows the user to select from preset film stocks
r, g, b StdDev	this value is multiplied by the amount parameter; a higher value indicates more variation in the grain, making it more apparent

Parameter	Function
r, g, b SpatialCorr	this value is multiplied by the grainSize parameter; a higher value increases the average size of the grain
r, g, b FilmResponse	inherits color from the input image instead of just black and white; for grain to appear more in the white areas, push it upwards towards 1
colorCorr	specifies the apparent colorfulness of the grain

6   Drag the Time Bar to view the composite.

The composite looks good, so it's time to make a flipbook—but not just any flipbook. Imagine a place where you could render a flipbook as a QuickTime movie, play it, and save it if you like it. Well, you've found it. On Mac OS X, you have an additional rendering option to render to a temporary QuickTime file. This allows you to play extremely long clips. Once this is rendered, you can then save the clip using QuickTime's built-in features.

7   Select Render > Render Disk FlipBook.

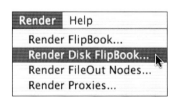

8   Select Render when the Flipbook Render Parameters window opens.

Shake pre-renders the QuickTime movie.

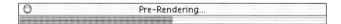

Once pre-rendered, the QuickTime movie is ready to play.

9   Click the play button at the bottom left of the Shake Preview window to view the QuickTime movie.

If you'd like, you can save the QuickTime movie from the Shake QuickTime Viewer File menu.

That's it. You can go home now.

10   Quit Shake.

What You've Learned

- You can apply a mask to any operation by dragging the output of a node to the right side of a second node. That node will only process within the white areas of the channel you specify.

- Animation is the process of setting values at various frames, or keyframes as they are called.

- With the FilmGrain node, you may apply grain from a preset film stock, match grain to an existing plate, or set your own grain by adjusting sliders.

6

Lesson Files	Lessons > Lesson06 folder
Media	bgd.1-10.iff
	final.1-10.iff
	wire.1-10.iff
	wall.tif
Time	approximately 1 hour and 30 minutes
Goals	Recognize the basic functions of the QuickPaint node
	Use QuickPaint to scrawl like a monkey
	Create a write-on effect
	Dustbust and Rotoscope a sequence of images

Lesson 6
QuickPaint

The QuickPaint function is a touch-up tool to aid you with fixing small element problems such as holes in mattes or scratches/dirt on your images. It is a procedural paint node that allows you to change strokes after they have been drawn. This helps us to emphasize its key feature: It is just another compositing tool that can easily be used in conjunction with other Shake nodes. This means that you can apply the effect and easily ignore it, remove it, or reorder it after you have applied your paint strokes. It is mighty handy, but it is not intended to act as a full-featured, paint-a-masterpiece paint package. Now that your expectations have been sufficiently lowered, you can begin.

The first input of the node is for the background and also acts as the Clone source. The second input is for the Reveal source.

Setting Resolution

You can apply a QuickPaint node to another node, or you can create a floating paint node that can be later applied to a different node with a Layer or mask operator. When the node is floating, it will take the resolution of the defaultWidth and Height.

> **TIP** ▶ A good way to set the resolution is to create an Image–Color node and attach the QuickPaint node to that. You would then set the resolution in the Color node. When you are using the Color node, keep in mind that the alpha channel is set to 1—which is completely opaque—by default. Keep your resolution in mind because QuickPaint does not paint beyond the boundaries of the frame.

1   Start Shake.

2   In the Image tab, select a QuickPaint node.

Edit versus Paint Mode

The QuickPaint node has a tool shelf on the Viewer, as well as three subtabs—Paint, Edit, and Globals—in the Parameters tab.

The first button on the Viewer is the Paint/Edit toggle.

When you are in Paint mode, you can apply new brush strokes, and the Paint subtab will be prominent in the Parameters tab. When in Edit mode, you can modify either your current stroke or any previous stroke.

You can control the paint characteristics (color, size, brush type, opacity, and softness), the position or shape of the stroke, or apply a write-on/off effect.

When you are in Edit mode, the Edit subtab will be pushed forward. If you switch to the Edit subtab, it will also switch to the Edit tab on the Viewer. The same occurs for the Paint mode, but you can also quickly switch into Paint mode by selecting a brush type on the Viewer.

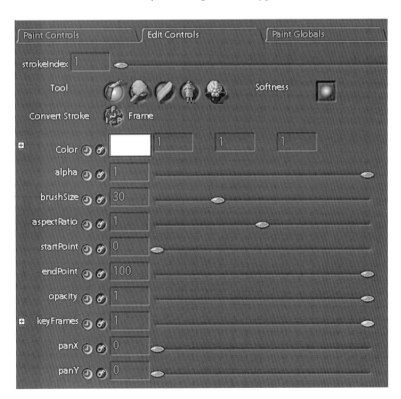

If you are in Edit mode, you can select any stroke to modify by clicking on the invisible stroke, which makes the stroke appear. You can also adjust the strokeIndex slider back and forth to expose previous strokes numerically.

Using the Brushes

The different brushes can paint on all of the image's channels at once or on the individual red, green, blue, or alpha channels separately using the R, G, B, and A buttons. For example, if you wanted to touch up only an alpha channel, you would turn off the RGB channels.

There are five basic brush types with one modifier to change the drop-off on any of those types.

The basic paint tools are as follows:

Button	Name	Action
	Hard/soft toggle	paints any brush type with a soft falloff; this isn't a brush—it just modifies other brushes; you can also press F3 to toggle this
	Hard/soft toggle	paints any brush type with a hard falloff; you can also press F3 to toggle this

Button	Name	Action
	Paint brush	applies RGBA color to the first input
	Smudge brush	smears pixels around; you should always use the hard setting for the hard/soft toggle
	Eraser brush	erases previously applied paint strokes only; does not affect the background image
	Reveal brush	exposes whatever is in the second image input; if no second image input exists, it acts as an Outside node, punching a hole through both the paint and the first input source
	Clone brush	copies from whatever is created by the paint node or comes from the first image input; to move the brush target relative to the source, use Shift-drag

TIP You can select your last brush type by pressing F1 when the cursor is in the Viewer workspace. With this, you can toggle through paint–erase–paint very quickly.

1 Make sure you are in Paint mode and select the Paint brush.

2 Okay, now you can paint. Just don't make a mess.

3 To control the brush size, use Ctrl-drag. You can set it numerically in the Parameters tab, as well.

If you draw like me, your screen probably looks like this:

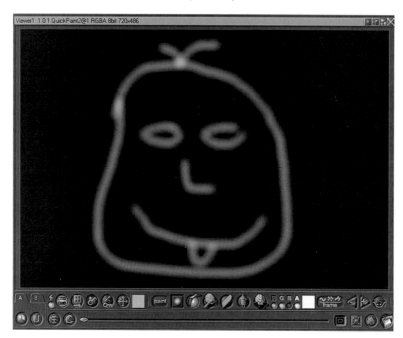

Some of you, no doubt, will already have a masterpiece on the screen.

Picking Color

You can pick your paint color and opacity several different ways.

In the Parameters tab is the Color Picker. Use it in the standard way to select your color, either from the Color Picker, by using the Virtual Color Pickers, or by picking from the image. You can also press F2 or P on the keyboard to temporarily jump into Color Pick mode.

NOTE ▶ The Color box on the Viewer indicates only the current color.

Modifying Strokes

You can animate strokes either by using the Interpolation or Frame setting, or you can modify any stroke after it has been made by switching to
the Edit mode. To switch to Edit mode, either press the Paint/Edit toggle
or go to the Edit subtab.

Once in Edit mode, you can select a stroke in one of three ways:

- Clicking on the stroke—The stroke will have an On-Screen control
  drawn on it.

- Selecting the strokeIndex in the Edit subtab—Each stroke is assigned a
  number, which can be accessed by the strokeIndex.

- Using the History Steps button—You can use these buttons to step
  backward or forward through your paint stroke history. This will not
  only select the stroke, but also draw up to that stroke. Even though the
  history list may contain later strokes, they are not drawn until
  you step back to them with the Forward History Steps button.

1   Toggle QuickPaint to Edit mode.

2   Click on the minus button of the History Steps button to cycle
    through your paint strokes.

    You can select knots or points on the stroke with the standard method
    of Shift-drag to add to your active knots or Ctrl-drag to remove from
    your active knots. You can also simply select a knot and drag it.

3   Select some of the knots on a stroke.

Once you have selected the knots, you can move them around and use the standard Autokey controls if you want to set keyframes. You can drag the knots in one of two ways. If you are on Linear Move mode, the knots will all move the same amount. If you are on Weighted Move mode, the knots nearest the cursor will move the most (this has no effect when only one knot is selected). You can also temporarily activate this mode by holding down the Z key and dragging. Using these tools, you can animate your strokes.

— Linear Move mode

— Weighted Move mode

4   Experiment with both Linear Move and Weighted Move modes while moving around a selection of knots.

If you want to insert a new knot, Shift-click on a segment. To remove a knot or knots, select them and press the Del key on the keyboard.

5   Shift-click on a segment to insert a new knot.

If you ever want to delete a stroke, you can do so by clicking on the Erase Last Stoke icon. Sadly, QuickPaint and Undo are not on good terms and, as a result, Undo does not work with QuickPaint. Thus, you have the Erase Last Stoke feature. You can also use the Edit subtab to modify your strokes.

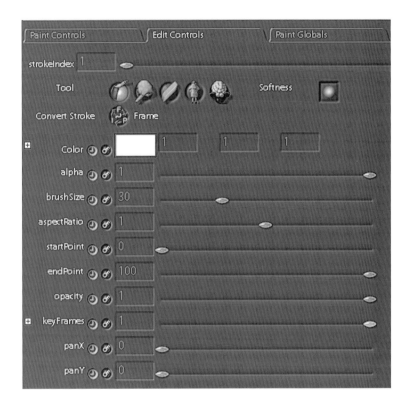

With the Edit subtab, you can switch the brush type simply by clicking on the Tool row of buttons in the tab. You can also change the softness. Additionally, you can alter the color, alpha, opacity, brushSize, or aspectRatio of the current stroke, all of which can also be animated.

6   Select the New Canvas icon to remove all strokes from your canvas.

If you can't see the New Canvas icon, you may need to expand the Viewer area.

Stroke Modes

You can use three different stroke modes while painting: Frame, Interpolate, and Persist. You will use these different modes throughout the course of this lesson.

- **Frame mode toggle**

  When you paint in this mode, you are painting only on the current frame.

- **Interp toggle**

  When in this mode, you can interpolate your brush strokes. Go to frame 1 and paint a stroke. Now go to, say, frame 20 and paint. When you drag back between 1 and 20 on the Time Bar, the stroke interpolates. If you go beyond frame 20 or before frame 1, the image is black. To insert a second interpolation stroke, toggle through the Interp toggle until you hit Interp again and use the strokeIndex slider to select the stroke you want to modify.

- **Persist toggle**

  This means the stroke persists from frame to frame. You can change it by going into Edit mode and animating it, but otherwise it will not change.

Converting Strokes

So far you have been painting in the Frame mode, which is the default. You can convert paint strokes in the Edit Controls subtab by clicking the Convert Stroke icon. For example, you can convert a stroke created in Frame mode to a Persistent stroke.

Interpolating Paint Strokes

In this example, you will create a paint stroke at frame 1 and another at frame 50 in Frame mode. The strokes will be converted to Interpolate mode, and Shake will transition from one stroke to another.

1 Click on the Paint brush icon to go back to Paint mode.

2 Make sure that Frame mode is enabled.

3 At frame 1, draw the number 2.

4   At frame 50, draw the number 5.

NOTE ▶ In these images, each number is drawn as a single paint stroke.

5   Click the Edit Controls subtab.

6   Click the Convert Stroke icon.

The Convert Stroke window appears.

7 In the Convert Stroke window, enable Interp.

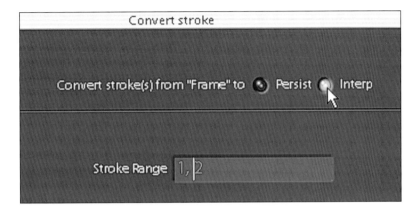

8 Enter *1, 2* in the Stroke Range field and click OK.

This instructs Shake to combine paint strokes 1 and 2 into one interpolated paint stroke.

9 Scrub between frames 1 and 50.

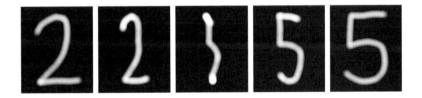

Shake interpolates the 2 and the 5 smoothly from frames 1 to 50.

10 Select the New Canvas icon to remove all strokes from your canvas.

Creating a Write-On Effect

Here's what you have been waiting for—an animated write-on effect.

1   Click on the Paint brush icon to go back to Paint mode.

2   Make sure that you are in Persist mode for this effect, because you want to animate the stroke over time.

Persist mode means that the stroke is active during the entire sequence, as opposed to Frame mode, where the paint stroke is active only on the current frame.

3   Write the word *Shake* with your neatest handwriting, making sure to write the entire word in one complete stroke.

Your handwriting should look something like this:

Okay, I failed my handwriting class. So what!

4   Toggle QuickPaint to Edit mode so that you can see the stroke.

The stroke is now superimposed over the painted letters.

The two parameters startPoint and endPoint determine the percentage point at which the stroke starts drawing and at which it ends. You can therefore make a stroke animate its writing by setting keyframes for the endPoint from 0 to 100 over several frames.

5   In the Edit tab, turn on the Keyframe toggle for the endPoint parameter at frame 1.

6   Set the value to 0.

7   Go to frame 50 and set the endPoint to a value of 100.

8   Drag your slider in the Time Bar.

You should see the word Shake animating. Now, make a flipbook to see it moving in real time.

9   In the Globals tab, set the timeRange to 1-50.

10   Click the Flipbook button, play the clip, and close when done.

It is a thing of beauty.

Painting in Perspective

Shake allows you to paint in perspective using a Transform–Corner Pin function in conjunction with QuickPaint.

1   Start by clicking on the New Canvas icon.

2   Click on the Paint brush icon to go back to Paint mode.

3   Select FileIn from the Image tab and go to the Lesson06 folder.

4   FileIn the wall clip and fit the image to the Viewer by using the F key.

5   Highlight the QuickPaint1 node and select a CornerPin node from the Transform tab followed by an Over node from the Layer tab.

CornerPin pushes the four corners of an image into four different positions.

6   Connect the wall clip node into the right input of the Over1 node.

Your tree should look like this:

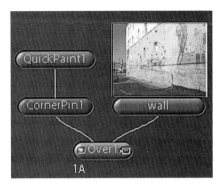

7 Click on the right side of the CornerPin1 node to edit its parameters.

8 Adjust the four corners of the corner pin so that they match the corners of the building.

The top-right corner of the building isn't visible, so you'll have to align the top of the corner by zooming out in the Viewer (– key) and pulling the upper-right corner far above the upper-right corner of the image. You can use the center line to judge the accuracy of your placement.

9 Click on the right side of QuickPaint1 to edit its parameters.

10 Make sure that you are in Paint mode and the Frame mode toggle is on.

Frame mode paints only on the current frame.

11 Use the F2 key to pick color off of the wall and proceed to paint graffiti.

You may have noticed that the profile of your brush has changed and is now vertically oval. The strokes that you are now painting are in perspective with the wall. How about giving the Clone brush a try?

12 Disconnect the **wall** clip from the tree and attach it to the left input of a new QuickPaint node.

13 Double-click on the QuickPaint1 node so that you can view and edit it.

14 Select the Clone brush.

The Clone brush will copy from whatever is created by the paint node or comes from the first image input. Shift-drag to move the brush target relative to the source.

15 Shift-drag to offset your paint source.

16 Clone various parts of the image using different brush offset settings.

17 While you're at it, experiment with the Smudge brush.

18 Make sure that the brush softness is set to the hard setting when using the Smudge brush.

19 Return the brush softness to the soft setting when done.

Dustbusting and Rotoscoping

Dustbusting and rotoscoping are two things that you will be doing a lot of, unless of course, you work somewhere that has an army of low-paid drones to do the work for you. Dustbusting is the process of painting dirt off of an image that was introduced by the film scanning process. Rotoscoping is a frame-by-frame, hand-painting technique to create imagery over time. QuickPaint can help you perform this otherwise thankless job of wire and dirt removal.

1 Choose File > New Script and answer No when prompted to save the script.

2 FileIn the **bgd.1-10#.iff**, **final.1-10#.iff**, and **wire.1-10#.iff** from the Lesson06 folder.

3 In the Globals tab, click the Auto button to the right of the timeRange button.

4 Click the Flipbook icon for each clip, starting with **final**.

The **final** clip is the finished shot. The **wire** clip is the shot you will be painting. It has a large crane and wire suspending a stunt man, as well as quite a bit of dirt. The **bgd** clip is a clean plate with no rigging. This

shot will be used as a source for the Reveal brush to get rid of any
unwanted objects in the frame.

5   Highlight the **wire** clip and select a QuickPaint node from the
    Image tab.

6   Connect the **bgd** clip to the second input of QuickPaint1.

7   Click on the Reveal brush.

The Reveal brush will expose whatever is in the second image input. If
no second image input exists, it acts as an Outside node, punching a
hole through both the paint and the first input source.

8 Make sure that you are in Persist mode for the first strokes you will be painting.

The crane on the left side of the screen and the stationary car in the foreground need to be painted out on every frame. In Persist mode, you can paint out these objects on only one frame, but the strokes will be drawn for the entire sequence.

9 Go to frame 10 and paint out the crane and tree on the left side of the screen, the car in the foreground, and the entire cloud area in the sky.

Since you are in Persist mode, you will only have to Paint these areas once.

10 Set QuickPaint back to Frame mode.

The remaining paint work you will be doing is on a frame-by-frame basis.

11 Go to frame 1 and paint out the remainder of the wire connecting the stuntman.

You might want to zoom in and center on the stuntman to see the wire more closely. In some cases, you may need to paint over your strokes several times to get adequate coverage.

12 Continue to paint out the wire on frames 2–10.

13 Make a flipbook of what you have done so far.

Hopefully, the wire and crane are gone and there is no flickering. Flickering is caused by strokes painted in Frame mode that don't completely cover the wire.

But what about the dirt—the small white flecks that appear in different areas of the frame? You will need to remove the specks using the same process outlined in steps 12 and 13.

14 Go to each frame that contains dirt and paint it out.

15 Make another flipbook.

If the wires and rigging are gone, if the dirt is gone, and if there is no flickering—congratulations. If not, you're not leaving until it is perfect.

16 Quit Shake.

What You've Learned

- Use Persist mode to keep the stroke over the course of all of your frames.
- Dustbusting is the process of painting dirt off of an image.
- Rotoscoping is a frame-by-frame, hand-painting technique to create imagery over time.
- The Reveal brush exposes whatever is in the second image input; the Clone brush copies from whatever is created by the paint node or comes from the first image input.

Keyboard Shortcuts

Paint

F1	last brush type
F2	pick color
F3	hard/soft toggle
P	pick color
Z	weighted move when in Edit mode

7

Lesson Files	Lessons > Lesson07 folder
Media	ship.1-30.iff
Time	approximately 1 hour
Goals	Draw and animate spline-based shapes
	Navigate the various functions of the RotoShape node
	Create multiple rotoshapes for a model shot

RotoShape

The term "roto" generally refers to the process of painting imagery or creating shapes by hand on a frame-by-frame basis. It is also synonymous with low-paid, tedious work. However, it is a very important part of the compositing process.

Shapes are often created on a frame-by-frame basis to extract or isolate a portion of the image. Shake's RotoShape node can create multiple spline-based shapes that can then be fed in as an alpha channel for an element, or they can be used to mask a layer or an effect.

RotoShape has many convenient features:

- You can create multiple shapes within the same node.
- You can have a soft-edge falloff that can be modified on a knot-by-knot basis for each shape.
- You can make one shape cut a hole into another.
- When you break tangents, they remain at the angle you leave them at until you modify them again.

NOTE ▶ Currently, the black holes will not punch a hole in RotoShape's alpha mask. This should be fixed in a future maintenance release. Therefore, if using this as a mask, either use one of the RGB channels as the mask or reorder the luminance into the alpha when using it with Inside or Outside. You can do this with Reorder–rgbl or a LumaKey at default settings.

Add Shapes Mode versus Edit Shapes Mode

1   Start Shake.

2   In the Image tab, select the RotoShape node.

    When the RotoShape node is active, the associated tools appear on the Viewer toolbar.

    There are two modes in RotoShape: Add Shapes mode (below, left) and Edit Shapes mode (below, right). You draw your initial shape and add shapes in the Add Shapes mode, and you modify or animate the shape in Edit Shapes mode.

3   Start by clicking on a blank spot in the Viewer.

    When you click on a blank spot, a new knot (or point) will append there. As you click, if you drag away from the knot, tangents are created.

4   Continue the shape by dragging away from the knots as you draw to
create tangents.

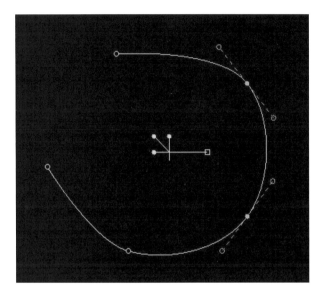

In Add Shapes mode, the shape does not render until you close the
shape.

5   To close the shape, click on the first knot that you added to the
Viewer.

When you are in Add Shapes mode, the shape will not draw (and will
therefore not affect later nodes). When you close the shape by clicking
on the first knot, you are automatically switched over to Edit Shapes
mode. In this mode, if you click on a blank spot and drag, you are
now selecting knots. Either drag to select a new group of knots,

Shift-drag to add to your group of active knots, or Cmd-drag to remove from your active group of knots.

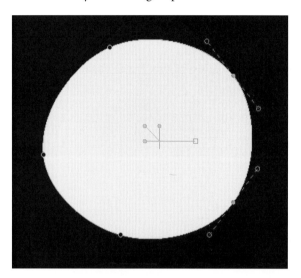

Inserting and Modifying Points and Tangents

1   Insert a new knot by holding down Shift and clicking on a segment area.

A new knot will appear.

2   Remove a knot by selecting it and then pressing the Del key or clicking the Delete Knot button.

You can modify a tangent in two ways: splined or linear. If you select it, you can toggle between Spline (below left) and Line mode (below right).

3   Select two knots and click on the Spline/Line toggle to the Line setting.

In this example, the two right knots have been made linear.

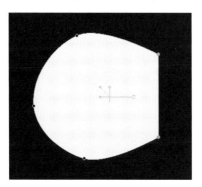

4   Toggle the Spline/Line toggle back to the Spline setting.

5   Try breaking a tangent by Ctrl-dragging on the end of the tangent:

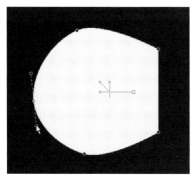   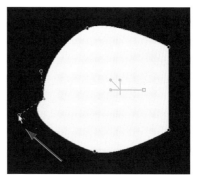

Ctrl-drag on the end tangent…   …to break a tangent.

Once it is broken, you can release the Ctrl key.

6   Drag one of the two broken tangents and you'll notice that the tangents are locked relative to each other.

To realign the tangents, hold down Shift and click on the tangent end.

Creating and Modifying Shapes

You can create additional shapes by clicking the Add Shapes button.

1   Click on the Add Shapes button.

This will slide you automatically into Add Shapes mode, and you can add another shape.

2   Draw another shape and close the shape by clicking on the first knot.

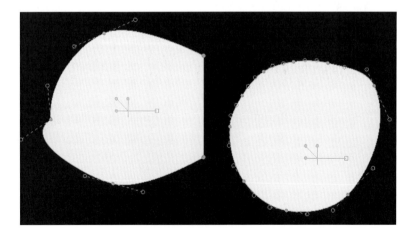

You can modify the shape by adjusting the transform control in the center of the shape. The small knobs going up and to the left are the Y and X scale parameters, respectively. The diagonal knot will scale both X and Y. The longer knob to the right will rotate it. Grabbing in the middle and dragging will move the shape.

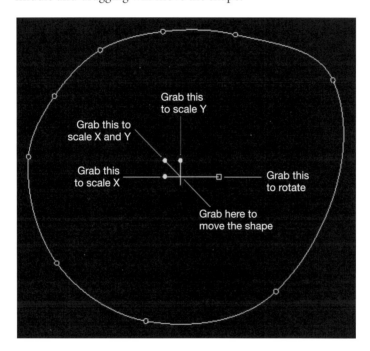

3   Experiment with the various shape transform controls.

TIP To move the transform control without modifying the shape, press Ctrl and drag with the left mouse button.

Knot Modes

Four different knot modes allow you to control the softness of a shape on a knot-by-knot basis, as described here:

Icon	Name	Hot Key	Notes
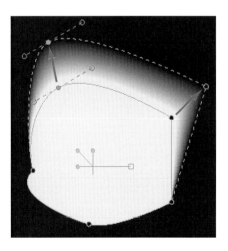 Group	Group mode	F1	moves both the main shape knot and the edge knot associated with it
Main	Main mode	F2	allows you to move only main shape knots; edge knots will not be modified
Edge	Edge mode	F3	moves only edges; you can therefore move the edge away from the shape
Any	Any mode	F4	allows you to pick any type of knot

1   To create a soft edge, click on the Edge mode icon and drag a knot out.

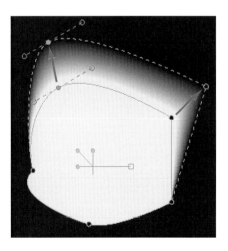

2   To reset the soft edge, right-click the edge knot and select Reset Softedge.

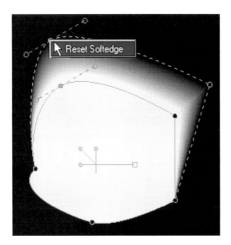

NOTE ▶ Be careful with the soft edges. If you make a shape where the lines overlap each other, you may get rendering artifacts. To clean up minor artifacts, apply a slight blur with the Blur node.

3   Go back to Group mode.

Right Mouse Controls

The right mouse menu on a knot or transform control gives you several other options, such as move controls to change a shape's layering priority, color options, the ability to delete a shape, and the ability to create parent-child relationships.

Right Mouse on a Knot

If you right-click on a knot, you will see the various controls.

The first one is the Bounding Box Toggle, which gives you a box that can be transformed to both move and scale the shape. You don't need to select this control; I just wanted you to know that it's there.

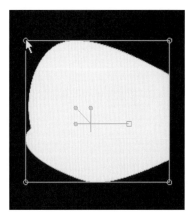

Another right mouse knot function allows you to specify a shape to be black, and then use it to punch a hole in other shapes.

1   Using the transform control, overlap the shapes.

2   Right-click one of the knots of the right shape and select Black.

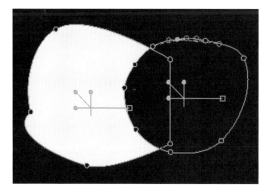

What do you know? The shape turned black.

The right mouse menu also has several Move functions, which can switch a shape's layering priority.

Right Mouse on the Transform Control

If you right-click over the transform control, you can set up a parent-child relationship between your shapes.

1   Set the right shape's color back to white and move it so that it is separated from the left shape.

2 Right-click over the transform control of the shape that you want to be the parent and select Add Child.

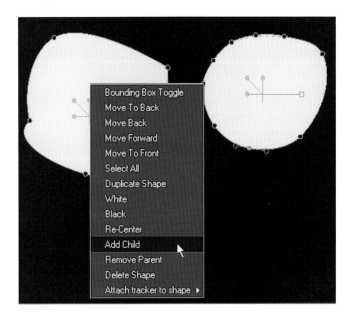

3 Next, click on the transform control of the shape that you want to be the child.

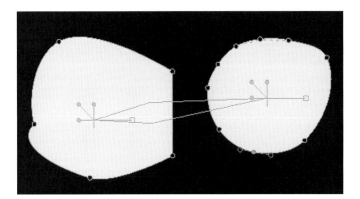

4   Now, move the parent shape, then move the child shape.

When the parent is moved, the child follows, but the child can have motion independent of the parent.

5   Remove the parent-child relationship by right-clicking on the child's transform control and selecting Remove Parent. (I wish I had that kind of control when I was a kid.)

> **TIP** ▸ You may find that the transform control might become uncentered from its shape depending on what actions you perform. If you right-click over the transform control of a shape, you can select Re-Center to center the transform control within the shape.

RotoShape Exercise

Your mission, if you choose to accept it, is to create multiple, animated rotoshapes so that the garbage surrounding the spaceship in the next example can be removed. The shapes that you create on a frame-by-frame basis will be used to place the ship on a uniform green background so that the ship can be eventually extracted and placed on a different background using a keyer. You'll learn about keying in Lesson 10.

1   Choose File > New Script and answer No when prompted to save the script.

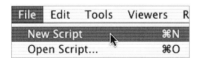

2   FileIn the **ship** clip from the Lesson07 folder.

Take a look at the **ship** clip in a flipbook.

3   In the Globals tab, click the Auto button to the right of the timeRange button.

4   Click on the Home icon at the bottom-right corner of the interface.

The Time Bar is automatically set to the Globals timeRange.

5   Click the Flipbook icon.

As you can see, the ship is suspended by a wire from above and a stand from below. The green screen is also too small to cover the entire area traveled by the ship. The first step is to create a loose rotoshape for the ship.

6   From the Image tab, select a RotoShape node.

7   Click on the left side of the ship clip so that you can view it while drawing the shape.

It will be helpful to set the resolution of the RotoShape1 node to be the same size as the ship clip.

8   In the Rotoshape1 node, set the width to 549 and the height to 467.

I have no idea how this clip ended up at this bizarre resolution. But hey, did I mention that Shake is resolution independent?

9   Go to frame 1 and turn on the AutoKey button under the Viewer.

TIP ▶ There's nothing worse than rotoing a shape and forgetting to turn on the keyframe button. Turning the keyframe button on will ensure that any changes you make to your shape will be animated over time.

10   Draw a loose shape around all of the unnecessary rigging.

11 Close the shape by clicking on the first knot.

Your shape should look something like this:

12 You will need to adjust the shape every five frames or so, keeping the rotoshape line outside the spaceship but on the green screen. Move to frame 6 and adjust the shape.

13 Continue to adjust the shape at frames 11 and 16.

You will need to refine the rotoshape starting at frame 18 because the ship moves off of the green screen.

14 Refine the rotoshape starting at frame 18 so that it exactly matches the edge of the ship where it extends beyond the green screen. You will need to change the shape on each frame from 18 through 30 to match the edge of the ship as it moves off of the green screen. See the following image.

You want to make sure that all nongreen areas are masked out by the shape.

15 Finish keyframing the first shape.

For your reference, or if you feel like cheating, I have prepared three scripts of this exercise at various stages of completion.

16 If you would like to see what I have done up to this point, select File > Add Script and select **ship_roto1.shk** from the Lesson07/scripts folder.

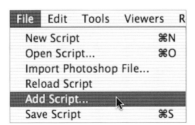

Add Script adds to your current script. In this case, one node called RotoShape_Pt1 is added to the Node workspace. Feel free to compare it to what you have done so far. Next, proceed with the more detailed roto work. You will create two new shapes that will cover the rigging above and below the ship.

17 Go to frame 1 and click the Add Shapes button.

18 Create a shape for the rigging on the bottom of the screen and close the shape by clicking on the first knot.

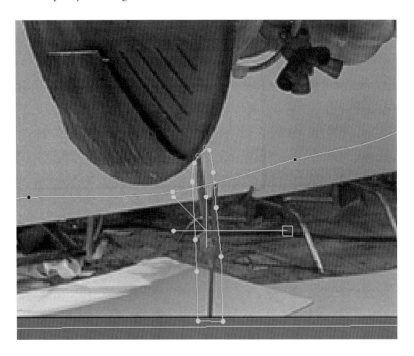

TIP ▶ If at any time the transform controls of a shape interfere with the editing of the points of another shape, move the offending transform controls out of the way by Ctrl-clicking and dragging them out of the way.

19 Click the Add Shapes button again.

20 Create a shape for the rigging on the top of the screen and close the shape by clicking on the first knot.

21 Continue to adjust the top and bottom shapes at various frames until all necessary frames have been adjusted.

22 Compare your roto to my version by selecting File > Add Script and selecting **ship_roto2.shk** from the Lesson07/scripts folder.

When you get to around frame 18 and later, you will notice that the top and bottom shapes intersect with some exhaust ports. In the following image, the white cursor is hovering over the lower one.

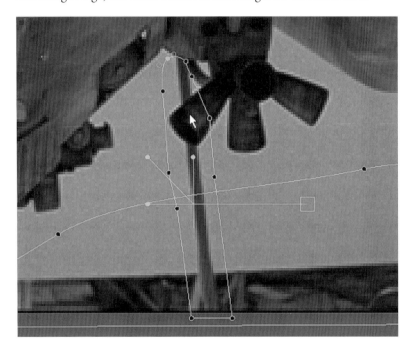

Rather than trying to roto around the exhaust ports, it will be easier to create a new, black shape that will knock out a hole in the rigging shape.

23 Go to frame 18 and click on Add Shape.

24 Draw a shape around the exhaust ports at the bottom of the ship and close the shape by clicking on the first knot.

> **NOTE** ▸ When you have multiple shapes that overlap each other, you may need to zoom in on the knots you want to move, especially if they are near other shapes or knots.

25 Fine tune the points so that the shape matches the exhaust ports.

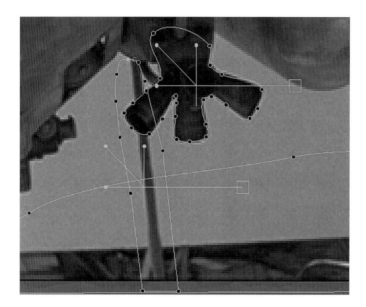

26 Click on the left side of the RotoShape1 node to view it.

27 Right-click on one of the knots of the exhaust port shape and select Black.

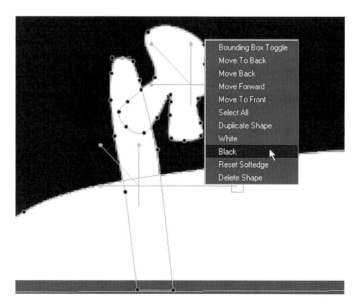

The exhaust port shape now knocks a hole in all other white shapes that intersect with it.

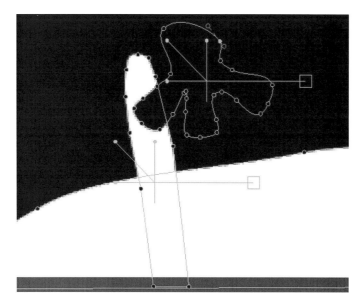

28 Go back to viewing the **ship** clip.

29 Animate the exhaust port shape during the time that it intersects with the rigging shape.

30 Create another black shape for the upper exhaust port and animate where necessary as you did with the lower exhaust port.

Okay, it is hours later and you are finished rotoing the ship using multiple shapes. To see how well you have done, layer the color green over the **ship** clip.

31 Highlight the **ship** clip and choose KeyMix from the Layer tab.

The KeyMix node mixes two images together through the specified channel (usually a mask) of a third image. You can control the mix percentage and also invert the mask. The ordering of the images in a KeyMix node are background, foreground, and matte.

32 From the Image tab, click on the Color node.

33 Connect Color1 to the middle input of KeyMix1 and hook RotoShape1 into the far-right input of KeyMix1.

Your tree should look like this:

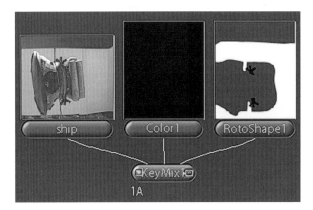

34 View and edit KeyMix1.

The composite is not working yet because black shapes in the roto-shape are not properly represented in the alpha channel. By default, KeyMix uses the alpha channel to control the composite, so it needs to be changed to one of the color channels.

35 Select G for the channel parameter.

36 Edit the parameters for Color1 by clicking on the right side of the node.

37 Click on Color1's Color Picker and then click on the green screen in the Viewer.

Your image in the Viewer should look like this:

38 Compare your final version with mine by selecting File > Add Script and select **ship_roto3.shk** from the Lesson07/scripts folder.

So, what do you think? Whose version is better? Well, thank you. I appreciate that. You are so kind.

39 Make a flipbook of KeyMix1 to see the result of your rotoshape animation.

Well, there you have it. The garbage around the ship is replaced with the green color selected from the Color Picker, and the ship is ready to be placed over a different background using a keyer. You'll learn more about keying in Lesson 10.

As a roto artist in training, you have gained valuable knowledge. You might even be able to make some money. RotoShape animation is an essential skill for every compositor; most large post-production companies have dedicated artists to create animated mattes.

40 Quit Shake.

Roto Tips

- View the clip and determine which frame will require the greatest number of knots to create the shape. Create the shape on this frame.

- Create as few keyframes as possible to animate the shape, but as many as needed so that the shape properly follows the object. For instance, on a 60-frame clip, start by adding keys at 1, 30, and 60. If you need more animation, add keyframes at 10, 20, 40, and 50. Continue to refine the animation by adding keyframes in-between to create an exact match.

- Creating too many keyframes can cause jittering in the shape.

- A Tracker, which is a node that analyzes the motion of a clip, can be attached to a shape. The motion from the Tracker is used to animate the shape's horizontal and vertical positioning. It sure beats animating frame by frame. To attach a Tracker to a shape, right-click on the shape transform control and select Attach Tracker to Shape. This calls up a list of pre-created Trackers for you to select from. Tracking is covered in Lesson 13.

Miscellaneous Rotoshape Viewer Controls

Button	Name	Action
	Toggle Fill/ No Fill mode	quickly toggle on and off the rendering of the shape
	Show/Hide Tangents	control the tangent visibility; when in Pick mode, only the active knot will display a tangent; none will hide all tangents, and All will display all tangents
	Lock/Unlock Tangents	lock or unlock the tangents of adjacent knots when moving any knot
	Enable/Disable Transform	a really annoying On-Screen control to pan the entire collection of shapes; it is off by default
	Key Multiple/ Single Shapes	indicates if you are keyframing the active shape or all shapes when you roto
	Toggle Path	if the main onscreen transform tool is turned on, this will toggle the visibility of the animation path; doesn't have a purpose if this tool is turned off
	Enable/Disable Shape Transform Control	turns the shape transform control on and off

What You've Learned

- Rotoshaping is a frame-by-frame shape-drawing technique used to create animated shapes over time.

- The Toggle Fill/No Fill mode button toggles off the rendering of shapes.

- The softness of a shape can be controlled on a knot-by-knot basis using four different knot modes: Group, Main, Edge, and Any.

- Create as few keyframes as possible to animate the shape, but as many as needed so that the shape properly follows the object.

Keyboard Shortcuts

Knot Modes

F1	group mode: moves both the main shape knot and edge knot associated with it
F2	main mode: moves main shape knots only
F3	edge mode: moves edge knots only
F4	any mode: allows you to move either the main shape knots or edge knots

8

Lesson Files   Lessons > Lesson08 folder

Media   vine_3d.1-80.iff

vine_3d_depth.1-80.iff

vine_bgd_bush.1-80.iff

vine_comp.1-80.iff

Time   approximately 1 hour

Goals   Create proxies, proxies, and more proxies

Integrate Kodak Cineon 10-bit log images into a composite

Create a composite at low resolution and then convert to
high resolution

Work with squeezed images and proxies

Film Compositing

In this module, you will create a film composite using low-resolution proxies to work faster and more efficiently. Once you're happy with the composite, you will switch over and work with the original, high-resolution film images.

This is the composite you will build in this lesson.

Film Resolution Files

Film resolution files are generally scanned at a size of 2048 × 1556 pixels. The large size of film images means longer processing and slower interaction. You'll see what I mean in a minute.

1 Start Shake.

2 FileIn the **vine_bgd_bush** sequence from the Lesson08 folder (Lesson 08/vine_bgd_bush/full_res).

vine_bgd_bush is a 1828 × 1556–pixel, anamorphic film file. The anamorphic film format is horizontally squeezed at the time of photography with a special lens. Later, the film is unsqueezed when it is projected, producing a 2.40:1 aspect ratio.

3 Click the Fit Image to Viewer icon in the Viewer.

4 Switch the Viewer to Scrolling Update mode.

This displays each line, starting from the bottom, as the image renders. This mode is good for slower renders.

5 Advance the Time Bar 1 frame.

Working with film resolution files is definitely slower than the clips you have been working with so far. They take longer to load and longer to process. Shake has a number of tools—namely, proxies—to speed up interaction when working with these larger files.

Proxies

Proxies are lower resolution images that you substitute for your high-resolution images so you can work faster. Because the images are smaller, you drastically decrease your disk-access time, your memory consumption, and your processing time. Naturally, your quality will suffer as well, which is why proxies are generally for testing purposes. Once you are done assembling your script with proxies, you return your script to full resolution to render your final output. You can also use proxies for temporarily viewing anamorphic images in a flattened or unsqueezed space.

In this example, you have the full-resolution image and a ⅓ proxy. In the following images, you can see that the proxy takes up one-ninth of the space, meaning potentially only 11 percent of the processing time, memory usage, and disk activity.

 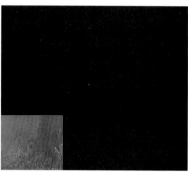

Full resolution   One-third proxy

Shake will automatically adjust pixel-based values to compensate for the lower resolution, so a Pan of 100 pixels is calculated to be only 33.333 pixels when using a ⅓ proxy. The actual Pan parameters in the interactive text field will not be modified.

There are three basic approaches for using proxies. These are controlled in the Globals section of the interface:

- **useProxy**

  You want to speed up your processing, but you don't plan on working on the project for an extended period of time.

- **useProxy + pre-rendering your proxy files**

  You are working on a project for a long time, the project is extremely large, and your high-resolution files are probably on a remote disk. You will be doing many flipbook tests.

- **interactiveScale**

  Your general speed is fine, but you want to adjust nodes quickly interactively at full resolution. This will not affect your flipbooks or renders.

On-the-Fly Proxies

On-the-fly proxies are generated only when needed and discarded when your disk cache is full. The disk cache is a temporary storage area on your disk used by Shake to improve system performance. The Globals useProxy parameter reads your input images and scales them down, placing them first into memory and then into the disk cache as memory runs out. It then recomputes the script at the lower values and leaves it at that resolution until you return it to full resolution.

> **NOTE ▶** The useProxy setting will affect your flipbooks and renders.

You can change to lower proxy sizes using presets.

1 Click on the Globals tab in the Parameters workspace.

2 Expand the useProxy settings.

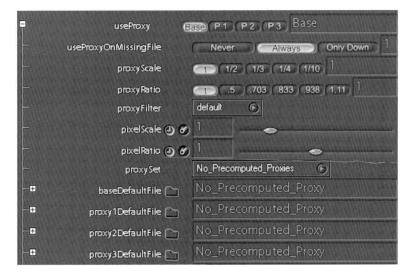

3   Cycle through the useProxy settings from Base to P1, P2, and
to P3.

By default, P1 is set to .5, 1 for its scale/aspect ratio; P2 is .25, 1; and
P3 is .1, 1. The current proxy setting will appear in the associated
text field.

Proxy Scale

Notice how the P1, P2, and P3 buttons automatically change the
proxyScale parameter. Shake automatically computes proxy images
based on a couple of Global parameters. The primary parameter is
the proxyScale variable. Not only will the proxy scale automatically
downsize all of your input images, it will also (behind the scenes)
multiply all pixel-specific parameters such as pan or blur values by this
same amount. The result is that you will end up with an image that is
visually the same, other than the quality difference, at both low and
high resolution.

When you activate a proxy, a proxy button illuminates at the top right of the title bar. You can use this button to quickly turn off proxies or return to any of the useProxy presets.

When generating proxy images on the fly, the following two things occur:

- All input images (such as FileIns) are zoomed down by the proxyScale amount. Thus, if your proxy scale is ⅓, all images are zoomed by one-third. When you change the proxyScale in the interface, you will notice that images in the Viewers all stay the same size on the screen. This is because Shake zooms the Viewer to compensate. The only thing you will notice is an apparent quality drop.

- These lower resolution images are stored to a cache on your local disk, usually the temp folder, as they are created. Thus, they are available whenever they are needed. Currently, these images are generated only when needed, so they're not created until you test a specific node. They also are generated only for the specific frame you are testing— when you move to a different frame, the proxies for that frame will be generated and cached. If you go back to the original frame, the proxies will already have been computed, and will be immediately available.

1   Temporarily set the proxyScale back to the Base setting by clicking the Proxy button once on the top menu bar.

Now you can test your images at full resolution. This temporarily turns off the proxies.

2   Click on the Proxy button once again to turn the proxies back on.

Keep in mind that using proxyScale is much different from simply appending a Zoom of the same value at the end of the script. The Zoom will calculate everything at full resolution and then perform the zoom-down at the end. Using proxies will pre-zoom all of the input images (which may take some time) but will then perform all further operations at this reduced resolution, which is usually much faster.

TIP ▶ Always remember to reset useProxy to the Base setting before you render your final elements.

Proxy Ratio

One other proxy-related variable needs discussing—the proxyRatio parameter. It is needed only if you are working with images that are squeezed, such as anamorphic film images. This parameter, proxyRatio, allows the proxies that are created to be of a different aspect ratio from the original source images. It specifies the width-to-height ratio (relative to the original image) that you want for your proxies. Thus, if you have an anamorphic film frame that is squeezed by two times along the X axis, you may want to set the proxyRatio to 0.5 to produce a proxy image that is unsqueezed or flattened.

1   Click on .5 in the proxyRatio parameter.

The anamorphic `vine_bgd_bush` clip is displayed properly as if it were projected in a movie theatre.

NOTE ▶ By setting the proxyRatio, you actually change the resolution of your image; it is not a visualization change. If you don't want to change the resolution of your image, you can change the aspect ratio of the Viewer instead of the image with the Global viewerAspectRatio parameter. This control is located in the Global guiSettings group.

2   Delete the `vine_bgd_bush` clip from the Node workspace.

3   Park the Time Bar at frame 1.

Customize P1/P2/P3 Settings

You can customize the P1, P2, and P3 useProxy parameters for your script or session by opening the desired proxyDefaultFile in the Globals tab and modifying the proxyScale and proxyRatio parameters. For example, I want

to have my anamorphic **vine_bgd_bush** image for my full-resolution file. I
want P1 to be ½ scale, but flattened (ratio of .5). I want P2 to be ⅓ scale
and also flattened.

1   Click on the Globals tab and change the proxySet parameter from
No_Precomputed_Proxies to Relative.

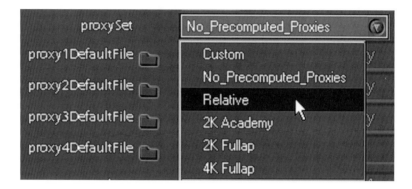

The Relative setting will save any pre-generated proxies in a folder
relative to your full-size file. This will make life easier when you get
to the next section—"Pre-Generated Proxies."

2   Expand the proxy1DefaultFile group.

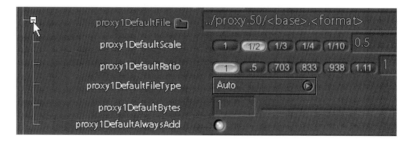

3   Set the proxy1DefaultRatio to .5 and leave the proxy1DefaultScale set
to ½.

4   Expand the proxy2DefaultFile group.

5   Set the proxy2DefaultScale to ⅓ and the proxy2DefaultRatio to .5.

6   Change the proxy2DefaultFile name from proxy.25 to *proxy.33*.

7   FileIn the **vine_bgd_bush** sequence again from the Lesson08/
    vine_bgd_bush/full_res folder.

8   Go back to the Globals tab and in the useProxy parameters, click on
    Base, P1, and P2 to toggle between the flattened and full-resolution
    versions of the file. Notice that the P1 and P2 proxies now appear in
    the corrected aspect ratio thanks to our customized settings.

Pre-Generated Proxies

Up to this point, Shake has been automatically creating low-resolution equivalents of your high-resolution source images on the fly. But you might want to use another method when you are working on a project for a long time and will be doing many flipbook tests. In this case, why not pre-generate your proxies when you start the project with an initial rendering process? The proxy files will then be pulled from these precalculated images rather than generating them on the fly.

You can either pre-generate the files inside the interface, or you can load them up after they have already been created by an external process. This is the workflow for generating proxies inside the Shake interface:

- Open the Globals—useProxy subtree.

- Open the desired proxyDefaultFile subtree and set your scale, ratio, format, and bit depth parameters for the proxy (like you did in the previous steps).

- Set your paths for where the proxies should go with the proxyDefaultFile setting. For instance, if you are using the proxySet:Relative setting, the proxy1DefaultFile default file path is ../proxy.50/<base>.<format>, which means they will go in a folder at the same level as the source images and be named the same name with the same frame range and in the same format.

    <base> = image name + frame range

    <format> = format extension

- Read in your images with FileIn.

- Select the FileIns for which you want to generate proxies.

- Choose Render > Render Proxies. From this window, you can launch a render of your proxy files. Make sure to activate the lights of the proxies you want to generate.

Okay, let's generate some proxies. The proxy settings you entered in the previous steps are fine. To recap, you set the proxy1DefaultFile to be ½ scale at a .5 ratio and the proxy2DefaultFile to be ⅓ scale at a .5 ratio. You also set the proxy2DefaultFile to a folder named proxy.33.

1   Highlight the vine_bgd_bush node.

2   Choose Render > Render Proxies.

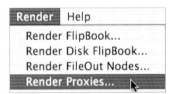

The Render Proxy Parameters window opens. Notice that all three Render proxyDefault parameters are turned off.

3   Click on the Render proxy1Default light to activate it.

proxy1Default is the only set of proxies that you want to generate at this time.

4   Enter *1-5* in the timeRange parameter.

5   Click Render.

Proxies are rendered into a folder called proxy.50 at the same folder level as the original images.

6   Activate the P1 useProxy setting.

A half-resolution, half-height, pre-generated proxy is shown on the screen. Yippee!

The Vine Composite

Let's start by creating the composite using low-resolution proxies. Out of the kindness of my heart, I pre-generated some proxies for you that are zoomed down by .3 with the anamorphic squeeze removed. You will be working with "flat" as opposed to squeezed proxies.

Getting Started

1   Activate the P2 useProxy setting.

The P2 setting will access the pre-generated proxies. Now, let's load the clips.

2   Switch the Viewer back to Normal Update mode.

3   Add a FileIn and browse to the Lesson08/vine_3d/full_res folder and double-click on the **vine_3d** clip.

4   Add another FilcIn and browse to the Lesson08/vine_3d_depth/ full_res folder and double-click on the **vine_3d_depth** clip.

5   Add one more FileIn and browse to the Lesson08/vine_comp/proxy.33
    folder and select P2 for the Load as proxy parameter at the bottom of
    the FileIn window.

Since the vine_comp clip doesn't have full-resolution images associated
with it, and since it is the same size and format as the P2 proxy set,
you can use the Load as proxy parameter to specify that this clip is a
proxy.

6   Double-click on the vine_comp clip in the FileIn window.

You should now have four clips on the Node workspace.

View the Clips

1   Automatically set the timeRange in the Global parameters by clicking
    on the Auto button.

2   Click the Home icon at the bottom right of the interface to set the
    Time Bar to the same time range.

3   Click the Fit Image to Viewer icon in the Viewer to reset the zoom of
    the Viewer.

4 Double-click on the **vine_comp** clip, click the Flipbook icon, and play it when it's done loading.

This is the final effect that you will be building. A computer-generated vine has been composited into the scene.

5 Load the **vine_3d** clip into a flipbook and play it.

The **vine_3d** clip winds through the image and also has an alpha channel.

6 Load the **vine_3d_depth** clip into a flipbook and play it.

This depth matte will be used for color correcting the **vine_3d** clip. Notice how the matte has gone too low at the top of the frame between frames 1 and 19. This will have to be repaired later on with a RotoShape node. This won't be the last time that you have to fix elements from the 3D guy. Get used to it.

7 Load the **vine_bgd_bush** clip into a flipbook and play it.

The **vine_bgd_bush** clip is a Kodak 10-bit Cineon log clip. In the title bar of the Viewer, it says that the clip is 16-bit RGB. Shake takes the 10-bit log clip and blows it out to 16 bit. It is still in log space and as a result looks washed out, because Cineon files are flattened out or compressed in the highlights and shadows.

8 Close all the flipbooks when done.

Kodak 10-Bit Cineon Files and Shake

Okay, time to take a nap—here comes some digital film history. Way back when, Kodak came out with the Cineon file format to support its film scanners and recorders. Because computer processors were slow and disk space and RAM were expensive, Kodak developed an efficient color compression scheme based on the idea that the human eye is more sensitive to low- and mid-tones than to highlights. These highlights can be compressed, saving the amount of data in the file. This resulted in a smaller, 10-bit file, making those old computer systems run faster.

Shake generally assumes that you are working in linear color space simply because mathematical operators will yield different results when working in logarithmic color space. It does not, however, necessarily mean that logarithmic images are not handled. If you exclusively bring in log images, the result will also be a log image. However, operations that involve multiplying or dividing (Mult, Gamma, Over, and so on) may return unpredictable results because values are being unevenly pushed in the higher or lower ranges. The preferred method of operation is to always convert your log files into linear space with the LogLin command before adding further operations. You would then continue with your compositing tree, until the end when you would place a LogLin command at the bottom of your tree to convert the image back to logarithmic color space.

That is about as complicated as this discussion will get. If you have some kind of masochistic streak within you, you can refer to the Shake Reference Guide for more information.

> **NOTE ▶** If you choose to do color corrections or composites in log space, you may have unpredictable results.

1   Attach a LogLin function from the Color tab after `vine_bgd_bush`.

LogLin performs either a log-to-linear or linear-to-log conversion. You can adjust the black and white points and gamma, and you can do color adjustments.

2   In LogLin1, change the DGamma parameter to a value of 1.

In most cases, you can ignore the DGamma setting, but for this image a value of 1 is best.

Adding the Vine

Since the **vine_3d** clip has an alpha channel, you can composite it into the background scene with an Over function.

1   Click on the **vine_3d** clip to select it and choose Over from the Layer tab.

2   Connect the output of LogLin1 to the second input of the Over1 node.

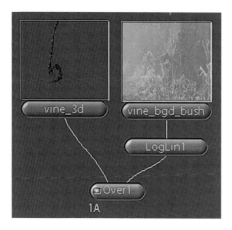

The **vine_3d** clip needs to be premultiplied by its matte, which can be done directly in the Over1 node.

3   Toggle the preMultiply parameter to the on position.

4   Drag the Time Bar to various frames to view your composite.

Color Correcting the Vine

The **vine_3d** clip needs some color correction to make it fit better into the scene. To start with, it is way too contrasty compared to the background.

1   Drag the Time Bar to frame 19.

2   Add a ContrastRGB node from the Color tab between vine_3d and Over1.

This applies a contrast correction on each individual color channel, so you can tune them separately. This differs from the ContrastLum function in that it changes only the pixel value according to its own channel.

3   Adjust the rValue, gValue, and bValue so that the top portion of the vine matches the background. For all you lazy types, the values I used are .828571 for the rValue and gValue and .836 for the bValue.

The top of the vine now matches the background where there is more smoke, but the foreground doesn't match. The **vine_3d_depth** clip will be used to color correct the vine more in the background than in the foreground.

4   Click on the left side of the **vine_3d_depth** clip to view it.

This depth matte was rendered from a 3D package whereby the values of the matte are based on their distance away from the camera. The darker the values, the closer the vine is to the camera. You can use this matte to constrain the effect of the ContastRGB1 node.

5   Click on the left side of Over1 to view it.

6   Connect the output of **vine_3d_depth** to the matte input of ContrastRGB1.

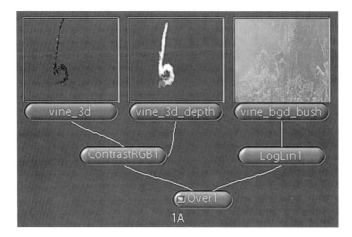

The ContrastRGB1 node doesn't seem to be doing anything now. Let's take a look at the Mask settings for the ContrastRGB1 node.

7 Click on the right side of the ContrastRGB1 node to edit that node's parameters.

8 Click on the + sign next to the Mask parameter.

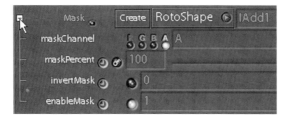

The problem here is that the Mask channel defaults to A for the alpha channel, which is a reasonable assumption, but not for this input clip, which has no alpha channel. The **vine_3d_depth** clip is a black-and-white matte in the RGB channels, so selecting any of the color channels for the Mask channel will work.

9 Change the Mask channel from A to G.

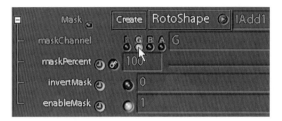

The vine is now color corrected more at the top of the vine than at the bottom.

10 Toggle the enableMask button on and off to see what the depth matte is doing. Leave the toggle in the on position when done.

Repairing the Depth Matte

Remember how the **vine_3d_depth** clip was messed up between frames 1 and 19? Well, now is the time to fix it.

1 Drag the Time Bar to frame 12.

Since the matte exhibits some rendering artifacts at the top of the frame, the color correction is missing in that area. An animated rotoshape will take care of this.

2 Click on RotoShape in the Image tab.

A RotoShape node is added to the page.

3 Click on the left side of the **vine_3d_depth** clip to see it in the Viewer.

The solution here is to draw a rough shape where the vine is missing at the top of the frame and will need to be animated between frames 1 and 19. First off, change the size of the RotoShape node to match the size of the **vine_3d_depth** clip.

4 In the width parameter, type *1828* and in the height parameter, type *1556*.

This sets the rotoshape to the same resolution as the clips you are working on.

5 Make sure that the AutoKey icon is turned on in the Viewer.

This will ensure that keyframes are set automatically each time you adjust the shape.

6 Draw a round shape at the top of the screen large enough to overlap slightly at the top of the vine.

7 Click the first knot that you added to close the shape.

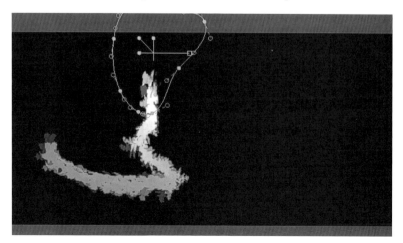

8   Use the On-Screen controls to adjust the shape on additional frames as needed so that your shape follows the top of the vine from frames 1 to 19.

TIP ▶ A fast way of scrubbing through your animation is to toggle over to Release or Manual Update mode on the top bar and then move the time slider. The shapes will draw in real time but will not be rasterized.

Adding the Rotoshape

Once you're done keyframing your shape, add it to the **vine_3d_depth** clip.

1   Click on the **vine_3d_depth** clip to select it and choose IAdd from the Layer tab.

2   Connect the output of RotoShape1 into the second input of IAdd1.

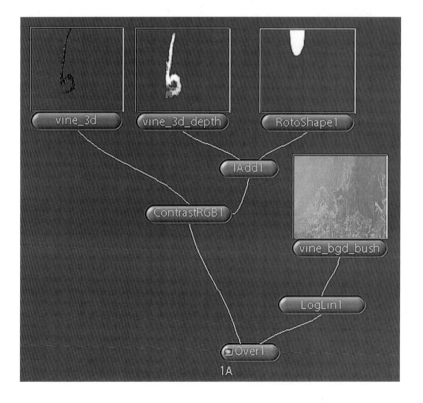

3   Click on the left side of IAdd1 to view it and drag the Time Bar between frames 1 and 19 to see your animated rotoshape combined with the vine.

This is probably a good time to view what you've done so far, but what do you do first? That's right, save the script.

4   Select File > Save Script.

5   When the browser opens, go to your Home directory and select the Shake_Output folder that you created in Lesson 2.

6   Type the name of your script in the File name path and click OK.

7   Double-click on the Over1 node and click the Flipbook icon.

8   Press the > key to play the clip. Close the flipbook when done.

The composite is on its way, but it would be more realistic if the vine cast a shadow onto the ground.

Adding a Shadow

You can add a shadow in a number of different ways. For this composite, you will use the DropShadow node. DropShadow takes an image's alpha channel and colors, blurs, and fades it to create a shadow effect.

1   Click on ContrastRGB1 to select it, right-click on DropShadow from the Other tab, and click on Branch.

2   Add a Move2D node from the Transform tab after DropShadow1.

The Move2D will be used to position and scale the shadow.

3   Place an Over node from the Layer tab after Move2D1.

4   Connect an output of LogLin1 to the right input of Over2 and connect the output of Over2 to the right input of Over1.

Your tree should look like this:

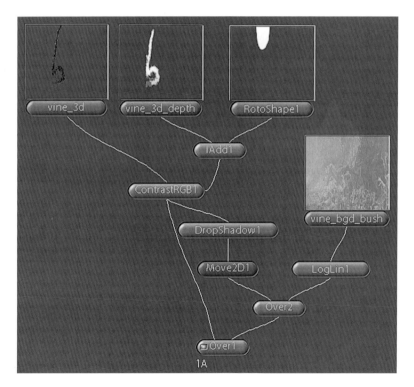

5 Drag the Time Bar to frame 12.

6 View the Over1 node and edit the Move2D1 node.

You can't see the shadow yet because it is in the same location as the original matte.

7 Set the xPan to -33, the yPan to -300, and the yScale to .5.

The DropShadow parameters could also use a bit of adjustment.

8 Click on the right side of DropShadow1 to edit its parameters. Set the fuzziness to 200 and the opacity to .4.

The fuzziness slider goes only to a value of 100, so you will need to manually type in a value of *200*.

9 Look at the Alpha channel in the Viewer.

Here you can see the drop shadow in the Alpha channel.

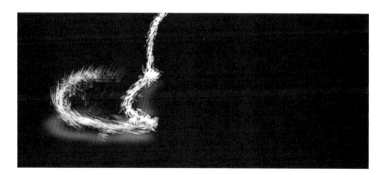

10 Now, view the RGB channels in the Viewer.

That's it; you're ready to look at what you have done.

11 Click the Save button above the Node workspace to resave your script.

12 Click the Flipbook icon and play the clip once it is loaded.

13 Close the flipbook when you're done.

Convert Back to Log Space

The last part of this process is to convert the Over1 output back to log color space. Remember back when you added a LogLin node to convert the **vine_bgd_bush** shot from log to linear color space? Now, you have to undo it and convert the entire composite back to log space.

1 Add a LogLin node from the Color tab after Over1.

2 Change the conversion parameter to lin to log.

3 Click the Save button above the Node workspace to resave your script.

Rendering Full Resolution

You now have a script based on using low-resolution proxies. Before the final render takes place, switch the Globals useProxy parameter to the Base setting.

1   Make sure that the Time Bar is parked at frame 1.

>   **NOTE ▶** If you don't perform the above step and are parked past frame 5, your nodes will turn red and no images will load. This is because there are only five full-resolution frames included on the DVD for reasons of space.

2   Set the Globals useProxy back to the Base setting by clicking the Proxy button once on the top menu bar.

The script looks exactly as it did before except now the FileIns have loaded the high-resolution versions and the final comp has an anamorphic squeeze. That's the beauty of this system. You can quickly work out your composite using lower resolution proxies and with the click of a button, switch back to your high-resolution originals. If this were a real job, you'd be ready to render. It's not a real job, so you're done.

3   Quit Shake.

What You've Learned

•   Proxies are lower resolution images that you substitute for your high-resolution images so you can work faster.

•   The proxyRatio parameter allows the proxies to be of a different aspect ratio from the original source images.

•   Kodak Cineon is a 10-bit logarithmic file format that uses an efficient color compression scheme based on the idea that the human eye is more sensitive to low- and mid-tones than to highlights.

•   The LogLin function converts logarithmic images to linear images and vice versa.

•   Always convert your logarithmic files into linear space with the LogLin command before adding further operations.

9

Lesson Files   Lessons > Lesson09 folder

Media   bee.1-16.rgb

boat_comp.1-70.iff

choppers.aiff

gun.aiff

Time   approximately 45 minutes

Goals   Illustrate the mechanics of video fields

Demonstrate the Shake workflow for video material

Open, play, and mix audio files

Video/Audio

This lesson introduces you to the way Shake handles audio files, video images, and in particular, video fields, interlacing, and field rendering.

These are two consecutive video frames split into four fields. Interlacing weaves fields together.

Video Fields

A review of the mechanics of video frames and fields is in order, so listen up. The resolution of video images is 525 lines for NTSC and 625 lines for PAL. NTSC video runs at 30 frames per second and PAL at 25 frames per second. Each video frame is made of two separate subframes called fields. Each of these fields is an individual snapshot in time. By using fields, the viewer sees twice as many frames and smoother motion. Even though the fields represent different points in time, they occupy the same video frame. This is achieved through a process called interlacing—the scourge of graphic artists and compositors everywhere.

The following pictures show two consecutive video frames with interlaced fields of a bee in motion. The more motion an image has, the more interlacing you will see.

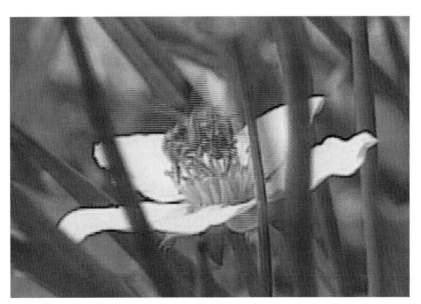

Frame 1

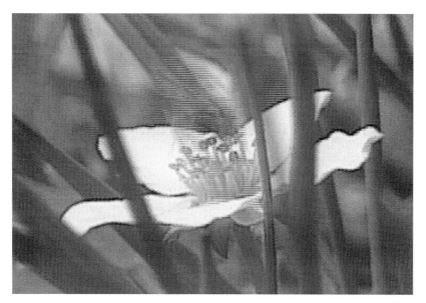

Frame 2

Here are the same two images split out into four fields:

Frame 1 Field 1

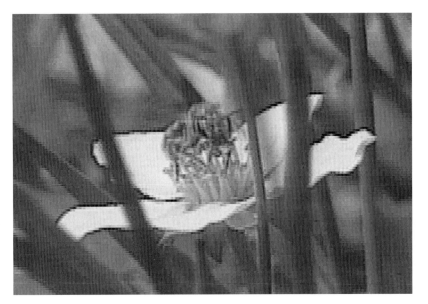

Frame 1 Field 2

Frame 2 Field 1

Frame 2 Field 2

Here comes the fun part. Interlacing weaves together the two fields by starting at the top of the image and taking one line from field 1 (the odd field) and another line from field 2 (the even field) until all 525 or 625 lines are interlaced together. Temporally, the fields always occur in the following order: field 1 and then field 2. Spatially, the ordering is different for NTSC and PAL. For NTSC, the spatial field order starts with field 2, or the even field. For PAL, it is the exact opposite with field 1, or the odd field, being the first spatial field.

Therefore, the interlace process produces two fields of half-height for every broadcast frame. When a television displays these images, it quickly shows the first field only, and then the second field only, and then proceeds to the next frame. This solution is interesting because each field sacrifices vertical resolution quality for the benefit of temporal quality.

Importing Interlaced Images

When importing interlaced images, you need to be aware of the FileIn node's deInterlacing parameter. When enabled, it strips out the two fields from each other, placing field 1 at frame 1, and field 2 at frame 1.5. Each field is then copied and moved into the empty spatial place of the removed field. This ensures that all spatial effects are properly handled when rendering fields. This strategy is clever because it doubles the number of frames you have, but keeps the frames within the same duration. Go figure.

1   Start Shake.

2   FileIn the **bee** sequence from the Lesson09 folder.

3   Set the Global timeRange to 1–16.

4   While you're at it, click the Home icon at the bottom right of the screen to make the Time Bar low and high values match the Globals timeRange.

5 Step through the clip with the left and right arrow keys.

Notice how the bee is interlaced as it flies.

6 In the FileIn parameter controls, click on the deInterlacing parameters until it says even.

Even is for NTSC and odd is for PAL.

7 In the Time Bar, change the Inc (increment) parameter from 1 to .5.

8 Step through the clip again with the left and right arrow keys.

You can now see the bee moving on each field in half-frame increments.

NOTE ▶ If you step through the animation and the image seems to stutter every other field, switch your deInterlacing to odd if you are on even and to even if you are on odd. The motion should then be continuous. Field order varies depending on the television standard; for instance, NTSC or PAL.

It is not always necessary to deinterlace video. However, it is helpful to deinterlace when you need to paint on individual fields, animate parameters, transform images, track motion, and create traveling mattes with the RotoShape node.

Common Problems with Interlaced Images

Interlacing creates two particular types of problems for digital image manipulation.

The first problem occurs when you have any animated parameter. The animation must be understood and applied at half-frame intervals. If you read in an interlaced clip and apply a static color correction, no problems occur because both fields receive the same correction. If, however, you animate the color correction, you must turn on the Globals: fieldRendering parameter in order to evaluate the correct set of lines at the appropriate interpolated value.

The second and trickier problem is with any node that has spatial effects, like a Blur or a Move2D. If you pan an image up by one pixel in Y, you have effectively reversed time, because the even lines are moved to the odd field, and the odd lines are moved to the even field. The clip would have extremely jerky movement, since every two fields are reversed.

Field Rendering

To correct the problems discussed in the preceding section, you can use fieldRendering in the renderControls of the Globals tab. With fieldRendering turned on, Shake separates the rendering into two separate fields. All animation and spatial effects are allocated to the proper fields. Why don't you give it a try?

1   Attach a Move2D node from the Transform tab to the **bee** clip.

2   Go to frame 1 of the clip and turn on the keyframe parameter for xScale in the Move2D node.

The yScale parameter is automatically linked to the xScale parameter because of Shake's default parameter linking. Therefore, it doesn't need to be animated.

3   Set the xScale parameter to a value of 0.

4   Go to frame 8 and set the xScale parameter to a value of 1.

5   Step through frames 1 to 8.

As you step through the frames, the Move2D animation that you created animates in half-frame increments. This is good.

6   Click on the Flipbook icon and view your animation.

The flipbook shows something quite different. There is only motion on the individual frames. This is bad. If you want to render on individual fields, you must turn on field rendering.

7   Go to the Globals tab and scroll down to the renderControls. Expand them by clicking on the + sign.

There are three fieldRendering settings:

▶   0 = Off.

▶   1 = Field rendering with odd field first. This is generally the setting for PAL images.

▶   2 = Field rendering with even field first. This is generally the setting for NTSC images.

8   Toggle fieldRendering until it says even.

9   Step through frames 1 to 8 again.

The Move2D animation is now field interlaced and will result in a nice smooth animation when it is placed back onto video tape.

You do not have to use field rendering when you import interlaced images and apply static color corrections. For all other functions, or if you animate any value, you should turn on fieldRendering. The fieldRendering handles all transformations, filters, and warps by internally taking each field, removing the intermediate black lines, and then resizing the Y resolution back up to full frame. Shake does this for each field and then interlaces them back together again.

Miscellaneous Video Functions

Shake has several other video-oriented functions. Keep in mind that these operate with the assumption that field rendering is off, since they would be affected by the field rendering options in the same manner as other functions. These functions include the following:

Tab	Function	Notes
Globals	dropFrame	toggles 30 to 29.97 frames per second when enabled
Time Bar	T on keyboard	toggles timecode/frame display
Image	FileIn	has de-interlacing, as well as pull-down/pull-up capabilities under the Timing subtab
Color	VideoSafe	this limits your colors to video-legal ranges
Layer	Interlace	interlaces two images, pulling one field from one image, and the second field from the other image; you can select field dominance; generally done with field rendering off
Other	Deinterlace	retains one field from an image and creates the other field from it; you have three choices on how this is done; the height of the image remains the same; generally done with field rendering off
	Field	strips out one field, turning the image into a half-height image; generally done with field rendering off

Tab	Function	Notes
	Swapfields	switches the even and odd fields of an image when fieldRendering is off; to do this when fieldRendering is on, just switch from odd to even or from even to odd; generally done with field rendering off

Audio

Audio normally plays second fiddle in most visual effects software and is generally referred to as the junk you drag along with the picture. Fortunately, Shake has some nice tools to handle this junk.

Shake can read AIFF and WAV files, mix them together, extract curves based on audio waveform, manipulate the timing of the sound, and save out the files again. These audio curves can be visualized in the Curve Editor.

NOTE ► Shake supports PCM AIFF and PCM WAV files. Although multiple frequencies and bit-depth importation is supported, playback is always 44.1 kHz, 16-bit at Medium quality, and export is always at Highest quality.

Loading and Playing Audio Files

1   Select File > New Script and answer no when prompted to save the script.

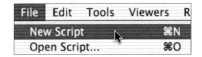

2 Click on the Audio Panel tab in the Node workspace.

The Audio Panel appears on the Node workspace.

3 Click the Open Audio File button at the top left of the Audio Panel.

4 When the File Browser opens, select choppers.aiff from the Lesson09 folder.

The choppers.aiff audio file loads into the Audio Panel and is ready to play.

5 Click the Preview Audio button.

The Preview Audio button plays the audio file and you should see the audio level displayed on the meters.

NOTE ► Because audio playback is handled through the use of Macintosh-specific QuickTime libraries, you can only hear audio playback on Macintosh OS X systems. However, you can still analyze and visualize audio on Linux systems.

Enabling, Viewing, and Editing Audio

Now that you have some sound, it would be nice to play with an image. It just so happens that there is a sequence of some helicopters that you can use.

1   FileIn the **boat_comp** sequence from the Lesson09 folder.

In Lesson 11, you will create the **boat_comp** from scratch, but for now you will use it for playback with the audio.

2   In the Globals tab, set the Time Range to 1-70.

3   Click the Home icon at the bottom right of the Time Bar to set the sequence to the Globals Time Range.

4   To activate the audio, click the Audio Playback button on the Time Bar…

…and click the play button to the right of it.

The audio and video play at the same time in the Viewer. The play-back speed will depend on the speed of your hard drive and the size of the image.

5   Stop the audio playback with the stop button to the right of the Time Bar.

TIP   You can scrub the audio at any time by Ctrl-dragging on the Time Bar.

Now that you can hear the audio, would you like to see it? The audio waveform can be displayed in the Curve Editor and slipped in time.

6   Click on the Curve Editor in the Tool tabs and activate the Curve Editor's Draw Waveform toggle.

The following image is an example of an audio waveform viewed in the Curve Editor.

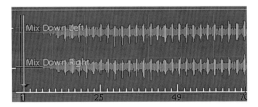

7   To slip all audio tracks in time, hold Shift+Opt and drag the mouse in the Curve Editor.

The audio channels are slipped in time.

NOTE ► You can also change the timing of an audio file by first making sure that it is selected in the Audio Panel and adjusting the Time Shift parameter.

Mixing and Exporting Sound

You can control how sound files are mixed together in the Mixdown Options subtree with the Audio Panel. Once finished, you can export the result to disk. Before you can mix audio, you will need to load another audio file.

1   Click the Open Audio File button at the top left of the Audio Panel.

2   When the File Browser opens, select **gun.aiff** from the Lesson09 folder.

Two audio files are now loaded in the Audio Panel.

3   Click the Preview Audio button to hear the two tracks at once.

The gun sounds a little too loud.

4   Enter a value of -8 in the Track Gain parameter.

Since the **gun.aiff** file is already selected, the Track Gain parameter will adjust only the gun sound.

5 Click the Preview Audio button again to hear your new mix.

Much better, because the gun sound no longer drowns out the heli-copters. If you wanted to save the mixdown to a new file, just open the Mixdown Options subtree and set the appropriate options—the most important of which are the filename and location for the new file and the Time Range. Once you click the Save Mixdown button, Shake renders out the new audio file.

Sounds good!

6 Quit Shake.

What You've Learned

- Each frame of video is made up of two separate subframes called fields.

- For NTSC, the spatial field order starts with field 2, or the even field. For PAL, it is the opposite: field 1, or the odd field, is the first spatial field.

- Shake can read AIFF and WAV files, mix them together, extract curves based on audio waveform, manipulate the timing of the sound, and save out the files again.

- You can change the timing of an audio file by first making sure that it is selected in the Audio Panel and adjusting the Time Shift parameter.

10

Lesson Files   Lessons > Lesson10 folder

Media   bg.1-78.rgb

bg_big.rgb

engine.1-78.rgb

gas.1-78.rgb

lens.1-78.rgb

parts.1-78.rgb

ship.1-98.rgb

ship_comp.1-78.rgb

ship_roto.1-78.rgb

Time   approximately 1 hour

Goals   Demonstrate the basic theory of the Primatte chroma-keying system

Change a clip from 30 fps to 24 fps

Use Primatte to generate keys

Keying

Keying and generating mattes is one of the most important aspects of compositing. The process of keying involves extracting an object from one image and combining it with a different background. Most keyers use the difference in color between the color channels of an image to extract the matte. Normally, this technique depends on the foreground subject being photographed in front of a uniformly colored background, such as a blue or green screen. Shake includes the Primatte and Keylight keyers, with the Ultimate keyer offered as an option.

Understanding Primatte

In this lesson, we'll use Photron's Primatte chroma-keying system. To effectively use Primatte, you need to understand the application and how it works. Primatte constructs a space described by three concentric partial spheres. The space is created by finding color values in a 3D axis, with each axis being a primary color of red, green, or blue.

These three shells separate four zones. Zone 1 is the complete background image. Zone 2 is the foreground image with spill suppression and transparency. Zone 3 is the foreground image with spill suppression. Zone 4 is the complete foreground image, 100 percent opaque with no spill suppression. As you scrub on an image, Primatte pushes and pulls on the shells based on which function you use, creating dents and bumps on the shells. The position of the dents is determined by the pixel values as located on the RGB axis.

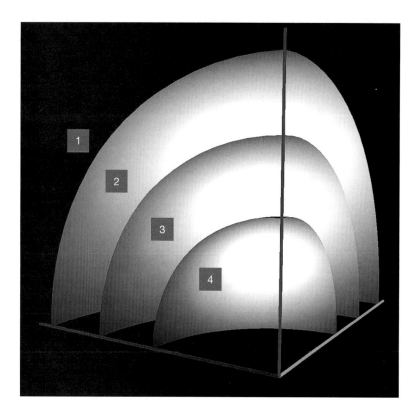

Visualizing a Primatte key in 3D color space would look something like this:

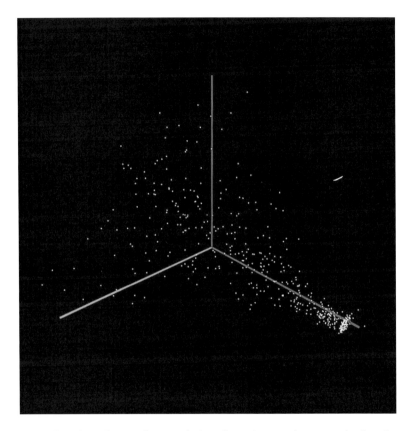

Pixels are distributed according to their color values and are manipulated based on their positioning within that 3D space.

Primatte Functions

Each Primatte function assigns pixels to a certain zone:

- **Background**

  When this mode is selected, the sampled pixels within the image window will be pixels known to be 100 percent background. The matte will be completely black.

- **Foreground**

  When this mode is selected, the sampled pixels within the image window become 100 percent foreground. The color of the sampled pixels will be the same color as in the original foreground image. The matte is completely white.

- **Fine Tuning: spillSponge**

  When this mode is selected, the cursor motion in the spillSponge slider performs a color adjustment of the sampled color against the background. After sampling a color region from the image, the further to the right the cursor moves, the less of the foreground color component (or spill) will be included in that color region. The further to the left the cursor moves, the closer the color component of the selected region will be to the original foreground image. This is similar to the more automatic but less controllable individual Spill Sponge operator.

- **Fine Tuning: fgTrans**

  This mode adjusts the transparency of the matte against the sampled color. After sampling a color region from the image, the further to the right the cursor is, the more transparent the matte becomes in that color region. This is equivalent to Make FG Trans but has more control.

- **Fine Tuning: detailTrans**

  This determines the transparency of the sampled color, which is closer to the background color. The slider in this mode is useful for restoring the color of pixels that are faded because of a similarity to the background color. If you slide to the left, picked areas are more opaque. This is equivalent to Restore Detail but has more control.

- **Matte Sponge**

  This is used to restore foreground areas lost during spill suppression. It affects only the alpha channel.

The following are more automatic but less controllable functions:

- **Spill Sponge**

  This affects the color of the foreground but not the matte. It suppresses the color you pick. This is usually used on spill areas that are known to be opaque, such as blue spill on the face or body. If the change is too drastic, supplement or replace the operation with Fine Tuning: spillSponge.

· **Make FG Trans**

This makes foreground material have more transparency and is used for adjusting elements such as clouds or smoke. It is the equivalent of Fine Tuning: fgTrans, except it has no slider control.

· **Restore Detail**

This removes transparency on background material. It is useful for restoring lost details such as hair. It is the equivalent of Fine Tuning: detailTrans but doesn't have a slider.

Viewing Your Clips

Before you begin, you'll need to load the clips.

1   Start Shake.

2   Select FileIn from the Image tab and go to your Lesson10 folder.

3   When the File Browser opens, press Cmd-A to select all of the clips and click OK.

This shot has quite a few clips, but you can start by viewing the final shot.

4   Go to the Globals tab and set the timeRange to 1–78.

5   Click the Home icon on the bottom right of the interface to set the Time Bar to the same range as the Globals.

6   Double-click on the `ship_comp` clip to select it.

7   Click on the Flipbook icon to play the clip.

For this shot, you will create a key of the ship and place it over the planet background. Next, you will integrate a number of computer-generated elements into the shot.

8   Close the flipbook and make a new flipbook of the **ship** clip.

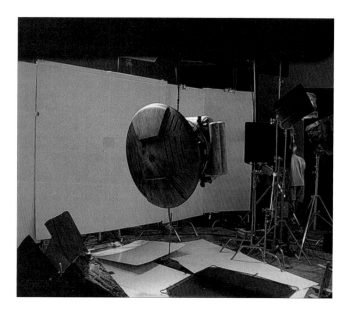

This is your green screen element. While playing it, you probably noticed some frames that have horizontal lines in areas of motion. This is because some of the frames are interlaced together as a result of what is called 3:2 pulldown. This pulldown is introduced during the film-to-video transfer process. In a moment, you will get rid of these extra frames.

9   Make a flipbook of the **ship_roto** clip, play it, and close the flipbook when you're done.

This is a premade garbage matte that will be used to get rid of unwanted items on the set.

10   Double-click on the **bg_big** clip to see it in the Viewer.

The **ship**, **bg_big**, and **ship_roto** clips are a higher resolution than the other elements. This is because a camera move will be applied to the ship, so it needs to be higher than the others. The **bg_big** clip is a single frame because it is used as a placeholder for the lower resolution, moving **bg** clip that will be added later.

3:2 Pulldown

What exactly does pulldown mean? It is a technique to temporally convert (resolution not being considered here) film footage to video footage and back again. Given that film uses solid frames and video uses interlaced fields, and that film runs at 24 fps and NTSC runs at 30 fps, you split the film footage into fields and double up two out of five frames to increase your frames to fill the 30 fps.

The pulldown parameters in the Timing section of the FileIn node allow you to manage the pulldown/pullup of a sequence.

30 to 24 (Pullup) means that you have received a film sequence that has been transferred at 30 fps. You now want to return it back to 24 fps. 24 to 30 (Pulldown) means that you want to take 24 fps film footage and convert it for 30 fps. Both allow you to select which field will dominate. Typically, PAL is odd and NTSC is even.

Here's the classic diagram illustrating this phenomenon:

Four film frames

convert to:

Five video frames

The third and fourth video frames have fields blending in them to stretch out time. It's therefore called 3:2 because you have three solid frames and two mixed frames.

You can fully reconstruct your original four film frames by extracting the field data from the five video frames. Here lies the wrinkle. When you receive your footage, it has probably been edited, so frames three and four aren't necessarily the mixed frames because all of the clips have been shifted around in the edit. You therefore need to figure out which is the first frame before you attempt to remove the extra fields.

To do this, go to your first five frames in the sequence. If the first frame to have field blending in it is frame 3, you know your firstFrame should be set to AA in the Timing section of your FileIn node. If the first frame to have field blending is frame 2, you know your first frame is BB. You would then set your firstFrame parameter accordingly. If your first frames have no motion or are a solid color and you just can't figure it out, you have to jump to a time range of frames that display the blending and start guessing what firstFrame is until the fields go away. Very scientific, isn't it?

NOTE ▸ You don't need to remove 3:2 pulldown from clips that were transferred from film to video. However, it is very helpful to remove pulldown when tracking, integrating multiple clips, or creating traveling mattes with the RotoShape node. Your workflow would be to remove 3:2 pulldown from all of your source material, composite the effect, and then add 3:2 pulldown to the final shot when done.

1   Double-click on the ship clip to load it into the Viewer.

2   Go to frame 59, where you can really see the interlacing of the frames.

3   Go back to the beginning of the ship clip and advance to the first interlaced frame.

The interlacing is a little harder to see at the beginning of the clip, but it becomes apparent at frame 3, especially in the items lying on the ground.

NOTE ▸ If the clip doesn't contain motion, you won't see any interlacing.

Frame 3 is the first interlaced frame. If you look at the diagram of the five video frames earlier in this section, you'll see that the first frame of this sequence would then be considered an AA frame.

4   Click on the Timing tab within the Parameters workspace and scroll down.

5   In the pulldown parameter, click on the 30 to 24 button.

This will convert your 30 fps clip into a 24 fps clip using the AA frame as the first frame in the sequence.

6   Load the ship node into a flipbook and click play.

3:2 frames are removed, changing the original 98-frame clip to 78 frames.

7   Close the flipbook.

Creating the Key

1   From the Key tab, right-click on the Primatte node and choose Create.

You probably noticed that the Primatte node has quite a few inputs.

Primatte Inputs (from left to right)

Parameter	Function
foreground	this is the blue or green screen image
background	this is the background image
garbageMatte	this is used to get rid of rigging or other elements you want to be transparent that are otherwise not pulled by the keying operation
holdoutMatte	this is a matte input for things that you want to be opaque
defocusedFg	this is used to take a blurred version of the blue screen to help deal with grain variation for film plates; typically, you would attach a Blur node to the blue-screen footage and insert it here

Primatte Inputs (from left to right) (continued)

Parameter	Function
replaceImage	you can do spill suppression with a solid color, with the background image (when no replaceImage is supplied), or with an alternate replaceImage to supply the color that will go into spill-suppressed areas; common inputs for this are bg, bg with Blur applied to it, fg with Blur applied to it, fg with Monochrome applied to it, or fg with AdjustHSV attached to it

2 Connect the **ship** clip into the far left input of the Primatte node and the **bg_big** clip into the second input.

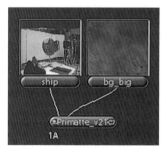

The Primatte node has a lot of parameters, so it's a good idea to change the layout of your interface.

3 Click on the dividing line between the Parameters workspace and the Node workspace and drag the line up to give yourself more room in the Parameters workspace.

The interface should look like this:

Now you can see all of the parameters without having to scroll the window. Primatte works by picking a Center value, meaning the average color of the key you want to pull.

4   In the Viewer, drag across a small section of the green screen.

Initially, nothing will happen, because Primatte is set to output the matte by default. If you are not viewing the matte in the Viewer, you won't see anything. If you want to see the composite, switch from Matte to Composite in the output parameters.

5   In the output parameter, select comp.

You can now see a preliminary composite that includes all of the items and rigging on the set. Don't worry about all of these extraneous set items, because you will remove them in a moment with a garbage matte.

6   Look at the alpha channel in the Viewer.

You will notice that there are gray values in both the ship and the background.

7 Click on the foreground button and drag across the gray areas of
the ship.

foreground

NOTE ▶ You may need to repeat this step multiple times until all of
the gray areas within the ship are gone by clicking the foreground
operator and then sampling areas in the Viewer.

This step tells Primatte to consider the gray pixels of the ship as foreground (opaque) material.

Since background gray values also exist, you should click on the
background button and drag that away as well. Do this even if you
can't see any impurity in the background. Your monitor will often
disguise noise hiding in the background.

8 Click on the background button and drag over areas of the green screen that are gray.

NOTE ▶ You may need to repeat this step multiple times until all of the gray areas within the background are gone by clicking the background operator and then clicking in the Viewer to sample. For foreground and background scrubs, you can drag as much as you want. For the other scrubs, use very fine, short scrubs.

Now, take away some green spill from the ship.

9 Look at the RGB channels in the Viewer.

10 Select spill sponge and scrub on the top of the ship.

Some, but not all, of the green spill is removed from the ship.

11 Use the active button to toggle the spill sponge on and off to see what it is doing. Leave the active button on when you are done.

You may want to use Fine Tuning: spillSponge instead because it gives you more control.

12 Click on delete op to remove the spill sponge operation.

13 Drag the currentOp slider all the way to the left.

Notice how you toggle through the operations you have already per-
formed. By parking the currentOp slider at a particular point, you can
modify, delete, or insert a new operation.

14 Drag the currentOp slider all the way to the right.

15 Select fine tuning and scrub on the bright green section at the bottom
center of the floor.

16 Move the spillSponge slider all the way to the right.

There is still too much green spill. Even though the slider is all the way to the right, you can enter a higher value in the spillSponge text box.

17 Type a value of 5 in the spillSponge text box and press Enter.

For now, the amount of green suppression is as good as it is going to get. Later, you will perform additional color correction outside of Primatte to remove the rest of the green spill.

Next, you need to remove all of the garbage on the set. The third input from the left on the Primatte node is the garbageMatte input. Plugging the premade **ship_roto** clip into this input will get rid of all unwanted areas on the set.

18 Click on the Node View tab so that you can see your clips.

19 Connect the output of the **ship_roto** clip into the third Primatte input from the left.

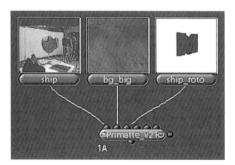

The unwanted areas of the set are still visible because the garbage matte input is expecting an alpha channel. **ship_roto** is an RGB-only clip, so the gMatteChannel parameter needs to know this.

20 Click on the G radio button in the gMatteChannel parameter.

All of the junk on the set is gone, leaving only the ship.

21 Click on evalToEnd to turn it off and drag the currentOp slider back and forth.

Turning off evalToEnd shows you the Primatte composite only up to the operation that you are parked on. This helps you examine all of the various steps that went into the creation of your key.

22 Click on evalToEnd to turn it back on.

Another useful Primatte function is the Status feature, which checks the values in your key. The Status output gives you a color code to determine where each of the pixels is positioned in the four Primatte zones:

23 Click the status button.

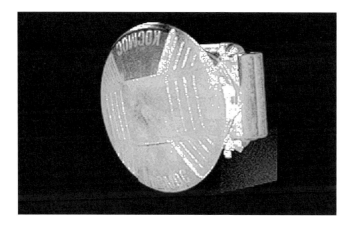

Primatte Zones:

▶ **Black Zone 1**
All background

▶ **Blue Zone 2**
Transparent foreground

▶ **Green Zone 3**
Suppressed foreground

▶ **Red Zone 4**
All foreground

Compositing the Moving Ship

The first part of this shot is almost done, but it needs a camera move added to the ship as well as further color correction and matte treatment. You should pull the matte on the full-resolution image before you do any scaling or transformations, using the appropriate output setting and doing the composite outside of Primatte. The output setting determines what is changed by Primatte:

- **alpha only**

    Primatte affects only the matte.

- **on Black**

    Primatte affects both the foreground image and matte.

- **comp**

    If you have an optional second input image, this will composite the foreground with the background.

- **status**

    This special output gives you a color-coded image to determine where each of the pixels is positioned in the four Primatte zones.

1   Click the on Black button.

    on Black will output the foreground along with its alpha channel.

2   Click on the dividing line between the Parameters workspace and the
Node workspace and drag the line down to give yourself more room
in the Node workspace.

The Lesson10/scripts folder contains a premade camera move for the
ship that you will load and integrate into the tree.

3   Choose File > Add Script.

4   When the File Browser opens, go to the Lesson10/scripts folder and
double-click on **Move2D_ship.shk**.

A node called Move2D_Ship is loaded into the Node workspace.

5   Connect the output of Primatte to the input of Move2D_Ship.

6   From the Layer tab, select an Over node and connect the output of the
bg clip into the second input of Over1.

The resolution changes to the lower resolution of the **bg** clip. This is
because Over1's clipMode defaults to the resolution of the background clip. This is good, because now that the ship has a camera
move applied to it, you don't need the extra size of the **ship** clip.

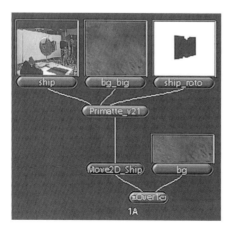

7   Click on the Flipbook icon and play what you have done so far.

The camera move created by the Move2D_Ship node gives the ship the illusion that it is rising in altitude.

8   Close the flipbook.

Now is a good time to save what you have done so far.

9   Choose File > Save Script.

10   When the File Browser comes up, go to your Home directory and select the Shake_Output folder that you created in Lesson 2.

11   In the File name path, type the name of your script and click OK.

Matte Treatment

The edge of the ship is slightly ratty, so you are going to work on its matte by eroding and blurring it.

1   Go to frame 58.

2   Highlight the Primatte node. From the Filter tab, add a DilateErode and then a Blur node.

DilateErode isolates each channel and cuts pixels away or adds them to the edge of that channel. It is good for either growing or shrinking mattes. For example, if you wanted to eat into your matte, you would set your channels to "a" for the alpha channel and then set xPixels and yPixels to a value of -1. In contrast, a positive value would grow the matte. By default, you are working on whole pixels, but you can switch to subpixel chewing by toggling on soften. Note that the soften parameter *really* slows the function down. We recommend low values for xPixels and yPixels if you are turning on the soften feature. When softness is turned on, the sharpness parameter controls how soft the edge is.

3   Click on the right side of DilateErode1 so that you can edit its parameters.

4   In the channels parameter, delete rgb so that only the letter "a" shows.

DilateErode will now affect only the alpha channel.

5   View the alpha channel in the Viewer.

6   Set the xPixels to a value of -1.

The yPixels parameter is automatically set to -1 because it has an expression that follows the value of xPixels. The DilateErode has chewed into the matte slightly.

7   Activate soften and set the sharpness to .5.

Soften activates subpixel erosion of the edge.

8   Click on the right side of Blur1 so that you can edit its parameters.

9   Set the xPixels and yPixels to a value of 3 and in the channels parameter, delete rgb so that only the letter "a" shows.

This softens the edge of the matte ever so slightly, but only in the alpha channel.

10   Double-click on the Over1 node and view the RGB channels in the Viewer.

Color Correcting the Ship

Now you need to color correct the ship to remove any remaining green spill in addition to adjusting its brightness and contrast.

1   Highlight the Blur1 node. From the Color tab, select the Saturation, Brightness, and ContrastLum nodes.

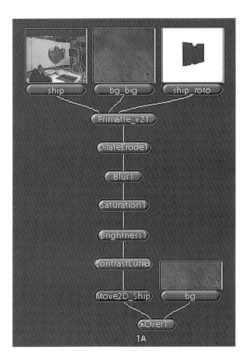

2   Click on the right side of the Saturation1 node so that you can edit its parameters.

3   Set the value parameter to .8.

The Saturation node helps remove any remaining green spill, but the ship could be darker and have more contrast.

4   Click on the right side of the Brightness1 node so that you can edit its parameters.

5 Set the value parameter to .8.

6 Click on the right side of the ContrastLum1 node so that you can edit its parameters.

7 Set the value parameter to 1.1.

The brightness and contrast of the ship more closely matches the background.

Adding Computer-Generated Ship Elements

You are now ready to polish up this shot by adding some computer-generated elements to the ship: a **gas** clip that wraps around the ship as it flies; an **engine** clip that generates a fiery exhaust and an engine glow; a **lens** clip that creates a lens flare as the ship comes closer to the camera; and a **parts** clip that explodes a variety of the ship's parts out into space.

> **NOTE** ▶ The motion of these elements has already been matched to the camera move that was applied to the ship using the Move2D_Ship node.

1 Load the **gas**, **engine**, **lens**, and **parts** clips into a flipbook and play them.

2 Close each flipbook when you are done playing it.

3 Go to frame 15, highlight the Over1 node, and add a Screen node from the Layer tab.

The Screen function mimics the effect of exposing two film negatives together. Technically, it inverts both layers, multiplies the two together, and inverts the result back. It is particularly handy for doing reflections and luminescent elements because it preserves the highlights.

4   Connect the **gas** clip into the second input of Screen1.

The gas is a little bit bright, wouldn't you say?

5   Attach a Brightness node between the **gas** clip and Screen1 and set the value parameter to .25.

Next, you can add the exploding parts to the ship.

6   Go to frame 25, highlight the **parts** clip, and add an Over node from the Layer tab.

7   Hook up the output of Screen1 to the second input of Over2.

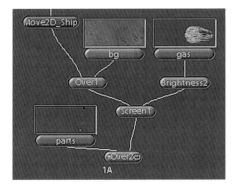

For a spaceship to look cool, it needs a fiery exhaust trail.

8   Add another Screen from the Layer tab after Over2 and connect the
engine clip to the second input.

The engine is partially over the ship now, but you can fix this by using
the matte from the Primatte key to put the engine behind the ship.

9   Take another output of the Move2D_Ship node and connect it into
the Mask input of Screen2.

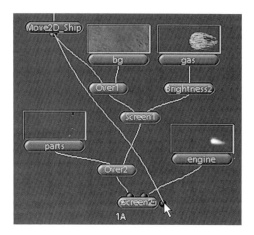

10   In the Screen2 node, expand the mask controls by clicking on the +
next to the Mask parameter.

11 Activate invertMask.

The engine is now behind the ship and looks pretty good.

12 Go to frame 74.

The engine is still behind the ship when it should now be in front. As the ship begins to turn between frames 70 and 74, you will need to animate the opacity of the mask using a Fade node so that the engine transitions from behind to in front of the ship.

13 Place a Fade node from the Color tab between Move2D_Ship and the Mask input of Screen2.

14 Make sure you are viewing the Screen2 node while editing the Fade1 node.

15 Click on the keyframe button next to the value parameter in the Fade1 node.

16 Set the value parameter to 0.

As you drag the value to 0, the engine trail connects properly to the ship.

17 Go to frame 70 and set the value to 1.

18 Step through frames 70 through 74.

The engines nicely transition from behind to in front of the ship.

19 Add another Screen from the Layer tab after Screen2 and hook up the
lens clip into the second input of Screen3.

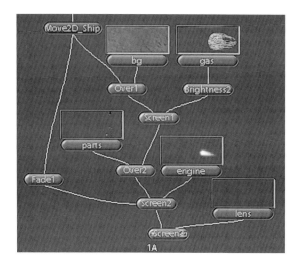

The lens flare is added to the engine, and the effect is ready to
preview.

20 Click on the flipbook icon and look at your masterpiece.

21 Choose File > Save to save your script.

22 Close the flipbooks and quit Shake.

Primatte Tips

- If you are having problems between the spill suppression, foreground, and background, move the Operator slider back to 0 to redo your initial Center pick. Click on the color box and make a much smaller drag of the background area. This way, all subsequent operations will be much finer.

- Foreground and Background scrubs can be as broad as you want. For the other color picking parameters, including the initial Center scrub, we recommend short scrubs, even as fine as one pixel.

- You may need to pull several keys (for example, one key for the body, one for hair, another for clothing, and so on). Use Primatte's matte arithmetic settings to replace, add, subtract, or multiply the foreground matte with the current Primatte matte.

- You can always leave the Primatte output on Matte and adjust the matte further with other tools such as DilateErode, Blur, Gamma, and so on, and then apply an MMult afterwards.

- Primatte does its spill suppression by pulling in color from the background image. The reasoning for this is that if a person picked up blue spill from a blue field behind them, then they would probably also pick up red spill from a red brick wall behind them. This means that sometimes the foreground will appear slightly transparent, even though the alpha channel is opaque. If you are having problems with this, use Primatte's replaceImage input. The replaceImage input allows you to use any image as the source for Primatte's color correction. Using a blurred version of the background in the replaceImage input is sometimes useful. Also, if a person is wearing a white shirt, you might want to set the ReplaceColor to white and activate use color for the replaceMode.

What You've Learned

- Primatte uses four zones to map out color values.

- 3:2 pulldown is a technique to temporally convert film footage to video footage and back again.

- Foreground and Background scrubs can be as broad as you want. For the other color-picking parameters, including the initial Center scrub, short scrubs as fine as one pixel are recommended.

- The spillSponge slider is useful for removing color spill.

11

Lesson Files Lessons > Lesson11 folder

Media background.1-70.iff

background_matte.0001.iff

boat_comp.1-70.iff

chop1_beam.1-70.iff, chop1_lens.1-70.iff

chop2_beam.1-70.iff, chop2_lens.1-70.iff

choppers.1-70.iff, choppers.psd

Time approximately 1 hour and 15 minutes

Goals Import Photoshop files into MultiLayer node

Stabilize shaky images

Animate using the KeyMix node

Use the Curve Editor to modify an animation

Use different image math functions and filters

Create a multilayer composite at video resolution

Advanced Compositing

The boat composite that you will complete in this lesson is an excellent example of how you would integrate multiple layers of computer-generated elements with a live action background. Often, computer-generated elements are rendered in separate passes to provide the compositor with ultimate control over the color, size, focus, and grain of the individual elements. This is the case here. So, ships ahoy my friend. It's time to combine all of the elements into one seamless composite.

Photoshop Files

Oftentimes, a visual effects supervisor previsualizes a shot that is created with Adobe Photoshop using embedded layers. This is done as an aid to the compositor so that they can realize the supervisor's genius. Shake can read Photoshop files in one of two ways. First, when a Photoshop file is imported with a FileIn node, you can read in a collapsed image, or select an individual layer. Second, you can import a Photoshop file as a script by using the File menu. Each layer becomes a unique FileIn fed into a MultiLayer node.

Importing Photoshop Files

1   Start Shake.

2   Choose File > Import Photoshop File.

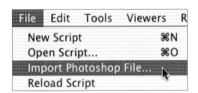

3   When the browser opens, select the `choppers.psd` file located in the Lesson11/multi_layer folder.

A tree is loaded into the Node View consisting of four clips plugged into a node named Composite.

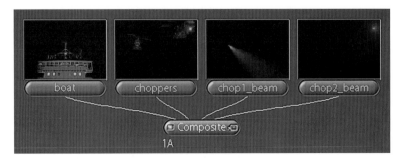

4   Hover your cursor over the Composite node.

At the bottom center of the screen, the Contextual Help window tells you not only that the node is named Composite but also that it is a MultiLayer node. It took the name Composite from the Photoshop file, but you can rename it.

5   Double-click on the Composite node so that you can see it in the Viewer and edit its parameters.

6   Rename the text in the MultiLayer parameter (at the top of the Parameters tab) from Composite to *MultiLayer*.

The MultiLayer node found in the Layer tab accepts an infinite number of input images, each layer containing its own unique settings to control the compositing mode, opacity, and channels. Because you may rearrange the layers via drag and drop in the Parameters tab, it also allows you to work using layer-based, rather than node-based, logic.

Take a look at the Parameters workspace.

Unlike other Layer nodes, the first input represents the background layer, the second input is the next deepest, and so on, until you reach the input farthest to the right, representing the foreground. When the nodes are inserted, they are stacked in the Parameters workspace as well, with the background at the bottom and the foreground at the top. Each layer has associated parameters and controls in the following order:

Parameters	Function
	shows the input of the image for that layer in the Viewer
	toggles the visibility for that layer
	solos the layer, making all other layers invisible
	turns off all layers above the current layer and keeps only the current layer and those below it visible
	dragging this icon changes the layer order
choppers	the name of the input image node; by blanking it out, the node is disconnected, but the layer information remains
PSScreen	the compositing operation for that layer
	deletes the current layer

Try out some of the layer functions:

7   Change the Compositing operation of the **chop1_beam** and **chop2_beam** clips to LinearDodge.

8 Toggle the visibility of the chop1_beam clip.

9 Solo the choppers clip.

Okay, so far you brought in a Photoshop file that automatically hooked up all of the inputs into your MultiLayer node. What if you wanted to add inputs to a MultiLayer node from scratch? All you have to do is drag the inputs into the + sign on the top of the MultiLayer node, which occurs when the cursor passes over it.

10 Choose File > New Script and click No when prompted to save the script.

FileIn the Source Material

1 FileIn all the files from the Lesson11 folder using Cmd-A and select OK.

You should have the following eight clips: background, background_matte, boat_comp, chop1_beam, chop1_lens, chop2_beam, chop2_lens, and choppers.

Take a moment to view the final composite before starting.

2 Pan the Node workspace and find the boat_comp clip.

3 Load the boat_comp clip into the Viewer.

4 In the Globals tab, set the timeRange to 1-70.

5   Click the Flipbook icon and play the clip once it is loaded.

What you have here are your standard computer-generated helicopters with light sources added to a live action background plate of a boat.

6   Repeat the previous steps to play the **choppers** and **background** clips.

Note that the **choppers** clip has an alpha channel and the **background** clip has camera weave as a result of being shot on 16mm film. This camera weave must be removed before compositing begins. The best way to do this is with Shake's Stabilize function.

7   Close all open flipbooks.

Tracking: Stabilization

Shake's Stabilize function uses a process called motion tracking. This technique involves selecting a particular region of an image and analyzing its motion over time. Once analyzed, the motion data is inverted and applied to the clip, causing it to become stable.

Shake has three tracking nodes: Tracker, Stabilize, and MatchMove. Tracker is a generic generator of an unlimited amount of tracking curves and is useful for passing these curves to the transform nodes. Stabilize removes bounce or jitter from a clip and can generate up to four trackers to be used in position, scaling, and/or rotational stabilization. MatchMove can track up to four points and apply the tracked motion of one clip to another. In this exercise, you will be using Stabilize, but the functionality is very similar between all of the tracking nodes.

1   Create a flipbook of the **background** clip again and zoom into the Viewer.

The clip's camera weave becomes pretty obvious when you are zoomed in. When integrating computer-generated images into a live action scene, it is essential that the background plate is stable.

2   Close the **background** clip flipbook.

3   Select the **background** clip and choose Stabilize from the Transform tab.

The stabilization track that you will be creating will be for position only, requiring only one tracker.

Stabilization Workflow

·   Play through your **background** clip several times to determine a good tracking point.

·   Attach your tracking Transform-Stabilize node to the **background** clip.

·   Make sure the On-Screen controls are visible in the Viewer.

- Go to the frame where you want to start tracking.

- Position the tracker at the point you want to track and adjust the reference pattern and the search region.

- Click either the backward or forward track button.

Positioning the Tracker

By default, the tracker appears in the Viewer. Each tracker has a reference pattern, search region, and track point.

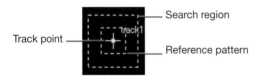

- **Reference pattern**

    The inner box is the reference pattern. It defines a small pattern that will be searched for in subsequent frames. It's always a good idea to choose a region with good contrast and detail. Corners with sharp contrast are usually good areas to track because motion can be detected easily in any direction. The reference pattern can be scaled to the desired size.

- **Search region**

    The outer box is the search region, which should be the maximum amount your tracking point will move between frames. The larger this is, the slower the tracker is. The search region can be sized in the same fashion as the reference pattern.

- **Track point**

  The center cross is the tracking point. It represents the position of the motion track. Normally, the track point is at the center of the tracker, but it can be offset if the reference pattern becomes obscured.

1 Make sure that you are positioned at frame 1 of the Timeline.

   If you click inside of the tracker, you will be moving the entire box.

2 Click inside of Track1 and position it on the center light under the top of the boat.

3 Zoom into the light by positioning the cursor over the light and pressing the + key five times.

4   Size the reference pattern (inner box) by dragging from one of the corners, leaving only a small amount of room around the light.

5   Size the search region (outer box) smaller, leaving a bit of room around the reference pattern.

Your track should look like this:

6   Press the Home button on the keyboard to zoom the Viewer back out.

Creating a Tracking Curve

When creating a tracking curve, you'll need to make sure that the trackRange, matchSpace, and subPixelResolution parameters are set properly.

- **trackRange**

  When you create a tracking node, the length of the input clip is automatically fed into the trackRange parameter of the tracker. The tracker will run from the current frame until it meets the range, either beginning or end, since you can track forwards or backwards. In this case, the trackRange is 1–70.

- **matchSpace**

  The matchSpace controls are located in the tolerances parameter group of your tracking node. Just click on the + next to tolerances to reveal the matchSpace parameters. When attempting to track a pattern, the pixels are matched according to the correlation between the selected color space, either luminance, hue, or saturation. By default, luminance is selected and will work well here because you are tracking a bright light.

- **subPixelResolution**

  Precision (and therefore time) of your track is determined by subPixelResolution, which is set to $1/16$ by default. For more precise tracks, lower this value. For this track, $1/16$ is fine.

- **Track buttons**

  The Track buttons are located under the Viewer when your tracking node is loaded into the Parameters workspace. The Track buttons start the tracking, going either backwards or forwards in time from the current frame. For this reason, you generally are positioning the tracker on frame 1 when you start. The tracker will go for the entire time specified in the trackRange parameter.

▶ Click the forward tracking button to start the tracking.

  Shake obtains the tracking data from frame to frame and stops when it gets to the end of the trackRange.

  NOTE ▶ To stop the tracker at any time, press Esc.

Apply a Tracking Curve

In this case, the default settings in Stabilize for applying the curve are set the way you want, with the exception of applyTransform. Remember, there are always exceptions. For different types of stabilization, you may want to change some of these settings:

- **trackType**

  Allows you to choose what track type you want, either 1 pt (panning), which is the default; 2 pt (panning, scaling, and/or rotation); or 4 pt (cornerpinning).

• **applyX/Y**

You can separately select applyX or applyY for panning, or you can select both (applyX/Y). Both are on by default, and applyScale and applyRotate will only show up in the menu if 2 pt is selected.

• **applyTransform**

The applyTransform function applies the transform needed to stabilize the image. It is inactive by default. You will need to turn this on.

1   Switch applyTransform to active.

2   While you're at it, click the Home icon at the bottom right of the screen to make the Time Bar low and high values match the Globals timeRange you previously set.

3   Double-click on the Stabilize1 node and click the Flipbook icon.

4   When it's done loading, press the > key to play the flipbook.

5   Zoom into the flipbook and examine the area that you just tracked.

The image should be nice and steady. Shake analyzed the motion data of the **background** clip and applied an inverse transformation to stabilize the shot. Isn't Shake great? It can do everything. It can even do your laundry.

6   Close the flipbook.

Building the Composite

Now that the **background** clip is stabilized, you can put together the rest of the shot. In this example, you are going to combine the choppers with the **background** clip using an Outside and an IAdd node—more on this in a moment. You will then add the chopper's light beams and lens flares together, also using the IAdd function. Next, you will add KeyMix nodes to bring the choppers and their lights from behind the ship to the front of the ship. Finally, you will use a Brightness node to color correct the choppers and add some rim light on the boat as the choppers fly overhead.

Adding the Choppers

The first step in this effect is to combine the choppers with the **background** clip. The choppers have an alpha channel, so you might say to yourself, "Self, put the choppers onto the **background** clip with an Over node." But you'd be wrong.

1   Go to frame 1 and look at the **choppers** clip in a Viewer and toggle between the alpha channel and the full color image.

If you examine the left chopper at frame 1 very closely, you'll see that the glow around the chopper's light is not included in the alpha channel. If you use an Over node, the glow of the lights will not be included. If you use an image math function, such as IAdd, to mathematically add the two images together, the glow will look right, but the choppers will appear too bright and transparent. Don't worry, there is a solution. Use an Outside function followed by an IAdd.

2   Select the Stabilize1 node and choose Outside from the Layer tab.

Outside places one image outside of the mask of a second image.

3   Connect the **choppers** clip to the second input of the Outside1 node.

The alpha channel of the choppers is used to "knock out" a black hole in that portion of the **background** clip.

4   Place an IAdd node from the Layer tab after Outside1 and connect the **choppers** clip to the right input of the IAdd1 node.

IAdd is an image math function that adds one image to another. In this case, the background clip that has the choppers "knocked out" in black is added to the full color choppers clip. As a result, the choppers and the light glow are both properly composited into the scene.

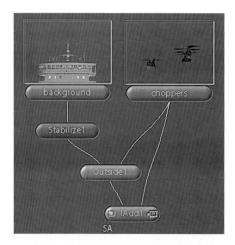

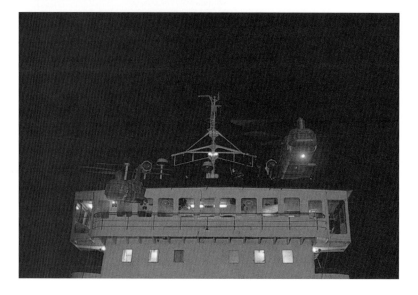

Renaming Nodes

You will use many similar nodes in the compositing of this effect, so you can rename some of them.

1   Double-click on the Outside1 node to view and edit its parameters.

2   In the Outside parameter of Outside1, type *chopper_knockout*.

3   Double-click on the IAdd1 node to view and edit its parameters.

4   In the IAdd parameter of IAdd1, type *chopper_comp*.

Adding Beams and Lens Flares to the Choppers

Next, you need to add the beams and lens flares to each chopper. Each exists as a separate clip, which you will combine with the IAdd node.

1   Move the `chop1_beam` and `chop1_lens` clips side by side, next to the chopper_comp node.

2   Load each clip into a flipbook and play them.

The `chop1_beam` and `chop1_lens` clips were rendered separately from the choppers to give you, the compositor, more control in the compositing process. Because they are separate, you can manipulate these elements independently of each other.

3   Close the flipbooks.

4   Select `chop1_beam` and choose IAdd from the Layer tab.

5   Connect `chop1_lens` into the second input of IAdd1.

6   Rename the IAdd1 node to *lights1_comp*.

Now, composite the lights1_comp with the chopper.

7   Add another IAdd to the Node workspace.

8   Connect the output of the chopper_comp to the left input of IAdd1 and connect the output of lights1_comp to the right input.

9   Select IAdd1 and rename it *lights1*.

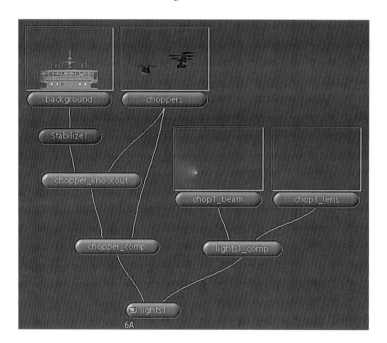

At this point you may need to zoom out on the Node workspace or make the workspace larger.

10   Select the `chop2_beam` and `chop2_lens` clips and move them side by side next to the lights1_comp node.

11 With the lights1 node selected, press Cmd-C to copy the node followed by Cmd-V twice to paste two copies.

Now, you have two more IAdd nodes to use.

12 Rename the lights3 node to *lights2_comp*.

13 Connect the **chop2_beam** and **chop2_lens** clips into the lights2_comp node.

14 Join the outputs of lights1 and lights2_comp into lights2.

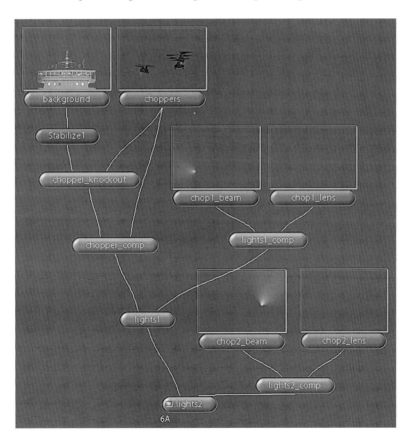

15 Double-click the lights2 node.

You see both choppers with the lights over the background.

16 Click the Flipbook icon and play what you have done so far.

17 Close the flipbook when done.

Adding More Layers

To create the illusion of the choppers and light beams moving from behind to in front of the boat, you need to add some KeyMix nodes to the tree. This effect is achieved by recompositing the ship over the background and animating the opacity.

Start by layering the choppers.

1 Select chopper_comp and insert a KeyMix node from the Layer tab.

The KeyMix node mixes two images together through the specified channel of a third image. The ordering of the images in a KeyMix node are background, foreground, and matte.

2   Connect another output of Stabilize1 to the center input of KeyMix1.

3   Look at the **background_matte** clip in the Viewer and examine the R, G, B, and A channels. Finish with the Viewer showing the RGB channels.

The **background_matte** clip is a black-and-white RGB clip.

4   Connect the **background_matte** clip to the right input of KeyMix1.

5   Double-click the KeyMix1 node to view and edit its parameters.

The composite is not working yet, because the channel parameter is not set correctly for the **background_matte** clip, which has no alpha. By default, KeyMix uses the alpha channel to control the composite, so it needs to be changed to one of the color channels.

6   Set the channel parameter to G for green.

The boat now appears on top of the choppers.

7   Rename the KeyMix1 node to *chopper_fade*.

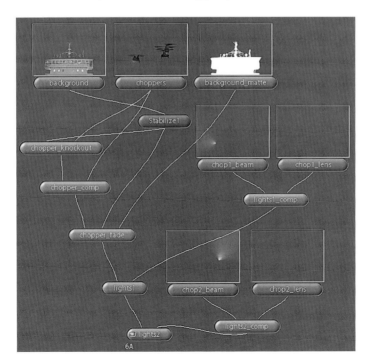

Animating the KeyMix

The following procedure places the choppers behind the ship for the first 34 frames and then performs a transition to put them in front of the ship's mast by frame 38.

1 Move the Time Bar to frame 34.

2 Turn on the Autokey for the percent parameter.

This automatically sets a keyframe at the current value of 100 percent.

3 Move the Time Bar to frame 38 and set the percent parameter to 0.

At frame 38, the choppers are in front of the ship.

4 Move the Time Bar to frames 1, 15, 25, and 42.

Notice how the choppers, especially the left one, start behind the boat and then end up in front.

Animating Lights1

The beams and lens flares need to transition from behind to in front of the boat with the choppers.

1 Insert a KeyMix after lights1.

2 Connect another output of Stabilize1 to the center input of KeyMix1.

3 Connect another output of the **background_matte** clip to the right input of KeyMix1.

4   Rename the KeyMix1 node to *lights1_fade*.

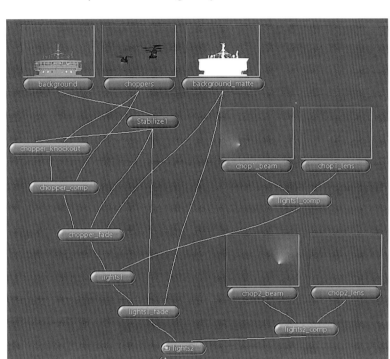

5   Double-click lights1_fade to view and edit its parameters.

6   Set the channel parameter to G for green.

The boat is layered on top of the beams and lens flares for the left chopper, but it needs to be animated.

7   Move the Time Bar to frame 33 and turn on Autokey for the percent parameter.

This automatically sets a keyframe at the current value of 100 percent.

8   Move the Time Bar to frame 43 and set the percent to 0.

This places the beams and lens flares for the left chopper behind the ship for the first 33 frames. After frame 33, the opacity changes and transitions the beams and lens flares to in front of the ship by frame 43.

9   Place your cursor over the Time Bar and using the left arrow key on the keyboard, step a frame at a time to frame 33.

Notice how the lights transition.

NOTE ▶ Stepping through each frame may take a few moments because each frame is rendering on the fly. After you have stepped through the frames once, they are cached on disk, and you can step through the frames instantly thereafter.

Animating Lights2

I'm getting kind of lazy, so rather than adding another KeyMix and starting from scratch on all the settings, I'll copy lights1_fade and modify it.

1   Click once on lights1_fade so that it turns green and press Cmd-C followed by Cmd-V.

TIP ▶ If you have a hard time remembering Cmd-C and Cmd-V, use the right mouse menu after selecting the node. From there, you can directly select the Edit > Cut, Copy, and Paste functions.

2   Double-click the lights1_fade2 node to view and edit it.

3   Rename it to *lights2_fade*.

lights2_fade carries all of the settings of lights1_fade—the node it was copied from. Once the proper clips are connected to it, you can modify the existing keyframes it contains.

4   Connect an output of lights2 to the left input of lights2_fade.

5   Connect another output of Stabilize1 to the center input of lights2_fade.

6 Connect another output of the **background_matte** clip to the right
input of lights2_fade.

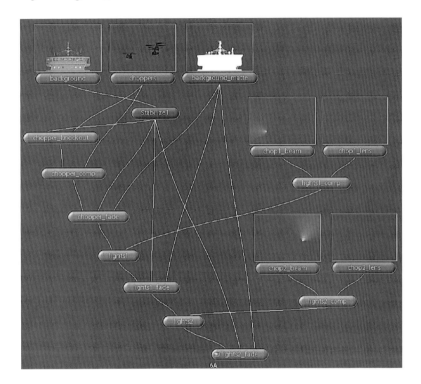

It's time to modify the animation of lights2_fade.

The Curve Editor

As you have been setting keyframes, these values are simultaneously being
entered as curves in the Curve Editor. Follow these steps to see what the
curve looks like numerically:

1 Click on the + to the left of the percent parameter.

What do you think of that? I know, you are feeling confused, yet impressed all at the same time. Well, you are looking at a numeric representation of the keyframes that have been set. It makes more sense now, right?

The Curve Editor allows you to visually see animated keyframes on a graph. You are able create, see, and modify these animation curves. To view the animated keyframes in the Curve Editor, click on the clock icon next to a parameter. When a checkmark is on the clock icon, it will be loaded into the Curve Editor.

2   Make sure that the percent parameter's clock icon has a checkmark next to it.

3   Select the Curve Editor in the Tool tabs.

The Curve Editor displays the animation curve for lights2_fade, lights1_fade, and chopper_fade. lights1_fade and chopper_fade are in the Curve Editor as a result of turning on Autokey while editing those parameters. You can turn off the visibility of these curves since you won't be editing them.

4   Click on the visibility icon (the V button) in the Curve Editor list for lights1_fade and chopper_fade so that the light next to each turns off.

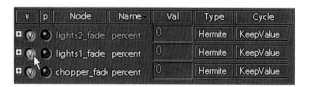

5   Click on the Home icon below the Curve Editor to center up the
     curve.

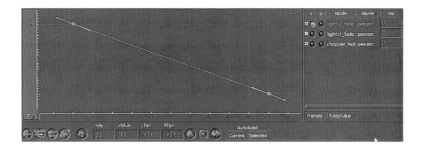

Take a deep breath and enjoy the beauty of the curve. All right, that's
enough, snap out of it.

Curve Editor: Adding / Deleting Keys
You can add keyframes on the curve by Shift-clicking on it.

1   Shift-click somewhere in the middle of the curve, and a keyframe will
     be created.

     You can either drag it around or, if it is still selected, you can enter
     numerical values in the text ports at the bottom of the Curve Editor.

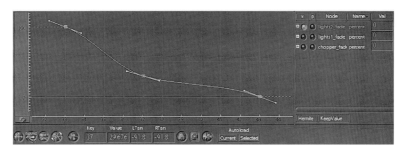

You can delete keys two ways:

▶ Drag a selection box around the key or keys and press the Del key.

▶ Move the Time Bar to where the key is and click the Delete Keyframe button if you are using an On-Screen control.

2   Drag a selection box around the middle keyframe and press the Del key on the keyboard.

Curve Editor: Selecting Keys and Curves

You can select curves and keys in several ways:

•   Drag the mouse over a segment to select a curve, or Shift-drag to add to a selection.

•   Drag over keys to select them.

•   Press Cmd-A to select all curves.

•   Press Shift-A to select all points on active curves.

•   Use the Curve List to select curves by name.

Curve Editor: Modifying Values

You can modify a value by:

•   Grabbing keys and adjusting their position in the Curve Editor.

•   Changing a key's value in the Parameters workspace or On-Screen controls when AutoKey is turned on.

•   Selecting the key and using the text ports at the bottom of the screen as virtual sliders (Ctrl-drag) to change the Key (its time) or Value.

Since this is a copy of lights1_fade, it has the same animation from frame 33 to 43. The value of these keyframes is correct for the new

node, they are just in the wrong place in terms of time. So move them,
why don't ya?

1   Drag a selection box over the keyframe at frame 33 to select it.

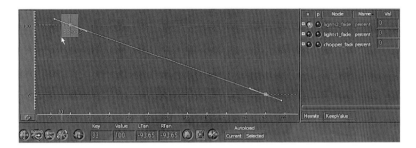

2   In the Key text port, change the value from 33 to 13 and press Enter.

The keyframe moves to the new destination.

3   Drag a selection box over the keyframe at frame 43 to select it.

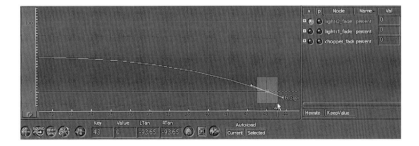

4   In the Key text port, change the value from 43 to 20 and press Enter.

The curve is no longer showing in the Curve Editor because it is in a different location in time.

5 Right-click in the Curve Editor and choose View > Frame Selected.

The curve is visible again and the keyframes are positioned properly for the right chopper.

NOTE ▶ At the end of this lesson is a complete list of Curve Editor keyboard shortcuts. For detailed information on the Curve Editor, please refer to the Shake Reference Guide.

6 Step through frames 13 through 20 and observe where the transition takes place for the right chopper's lights as it moves from behind to in front of the boat.

7 Click the Flipbook icon and play what you have done so far.

8 Close the flipbook when done.

The choppers and their lights successfully transition from behind to in front of the boat.

Edge Highlighting

To finish, you will illuminate the edges of the ship as the right chopper sweeps its light downwards using an Emboss, IMult, and an IAdd. To start with, you need to create an edge matte.

1   Drag the Time Bar to frame 28.

2   Right-click on the Convolve function in the Filter tab and select Create.

This adds an unconnected Convolve node to the Node workspace.

3   Connect the output of the **background_matte** clip to the input of Convolve1.

Convolve allows you to use a custom filter or to select from the Standard filters, consisting of sharpen, edge3x3, edge5x5, edge3x3, smoothedge, blur3x3, blur5x5, and laplace.

4   Click in the kernel drop box and select edge5x5.

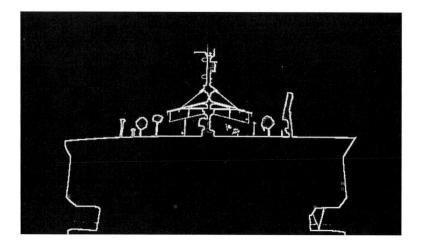

This creates a nifty edge matte based on the original matte. This is almost what you want, but what you really need is an edge matte that is only on the right side of the boat's surface. This way the light will be motivated by the right chopper. You'll see what I mean in a moment.

5   Replace Convolve1 with an Emboss function from the Filter tab.

Emboss allows you to create a simulated 3D effect. You control the amount of the emboss with the gain parameter and the light direction with the azimuth control. The elevation parameter is the "height" of the light. 0 means parallel to the image; 90 means the same axis as a line from your nose to the image.

6   Set the elevation parameter to 0.

You have a good edge matte now that is lit up only from the right side, but it needs a little bit of blur.

7   Insert a Blur from the Filter tab after Emboss1 and set the xPixels to a value of 8.

The yPixels are automatically set to the same value as the xPixels as a result of Shake's default parameter linking.

It's time to use this edge matte to brighten the boat.

8 Place an IAdd node from the Layer tab after lights2_fade.

9 Rename IAdd1 to *edge_light*.

10 Connect Blur1 to the second input of edge_light.

Okay, it's a little bright and the edge covers the entire length of the boat. It would be better if it only occurred in the area of the right chopper's light. An IMult would be good for this.

11 Add an IMult node from the Layer tab after Blur1.

This image math function multiplies one image by another, producing a result where there are values in both images.

12 Connect an output of `chop2_beam` into the second input of IMult1.

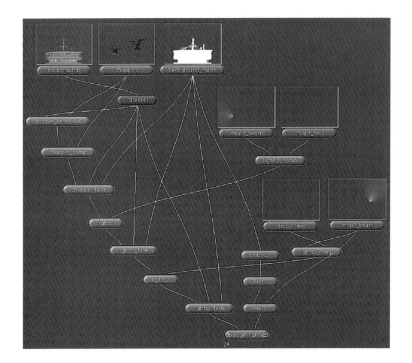

The boat edge lights up only where the light beam crosses the boat. It would probably be good to use the Compare function to see what is happening.

13 Click on the B buffer and then double-click on lights2_fade.

14 Click on the A buffer and then double-click on edge_light.

15 Click on the Compare icon once so that it is in vertical mode and drag the tiny, little C icon under the Viewer to compare the before and after.

This is looking good. It just needs to be animated up and down to follow the timing of the light beam.

16 Turn off the Compare function by Shift-clicking it once.

Shift-clicking takes the Compare function back one setting.

17 Drag the Time Bar to frame 25 and turn Autokey on for the edge_light percent parameter.

This will set a keyframe at frame 25 at a value of 100.

18 Go to frame 19 and 30 and set the percent to 0.

It's time to save the script and preview the effect.

19 Choose File > Save Script.

20 Navigate to your Home directory and select the Shake_Output folder you created in Lesson 2.

NOTE ▶ You should have created the Shake_Output folder in Lesson 2. If you didn't create the folder before, just create a Shake_Output folder within your user folder now.

21 Type in the name of your script in the File name box, and press Enter.

22 Double-click the edge_light node, click the Flipbook icon, and play what you have done so far.

You're almost done. Only one more tweak is needed.

23 Close the flipbook when done.

Adjusting the Brightness of the Choppers

As you can see, the choppers are too bright compared to the background. You will use the Brightness function to darken the choppers.

1 Select the **choppers** clip and choose Brightness from the Color tab.

2 You should be viewing the edge_light node while editing the Brightness1 node.

3 Set the value parameter to .75.

This darkens the choppers, and you're ready to render the effect to disk.

4 Select the edge_light node and choose FileOut from the Image tab.

5 Navigate to the Shake_Output folder.

6 In the File name box, type *boat_comp.#.iff*.

7 Click Render: Render FileOut Nodes from the pull-down menu and select Render.

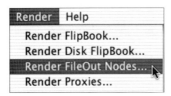

A Monitor window will appear to show you the progress of your render. Unlike a normal flipbook, only the current frame is loaded into memory. Previous frames are discarded from the Monitor window. Additionally, the Monitor window is always the same resolution, regardless of the output resolution settings. When the render finishes, you can load the frames up in a flipbook to see them.

8   When the render is done, close the monitor window.

9   Open up a new FileIn node and select the **boat_comp** sequence you just rendered.

> **NOTE** ▶ If you don't see your rendered sequence in the File browser, click the Force Update icon at the top right of the File browser.

10 Click the Flipbook icon to load the **boat_comp** clip and play it.

11 Click the Save button above the Node workspace to save the script.

You've successfully completed a fairly complicated multilayer composite. Pat yourself on the back.

12 Quit Shake.

What You've Learned

- Tracker, Stabilize, and MatchMove are Shake's three tracking nodes.

- The reference pattern defines a small pattern that will be searched for in subsequent frames; the search region is the maximum amount your tracking point will move between frames.

- Use the Convolve function to create edge mattes.

Keyboard Shortcuts

Curve Editor

Option-drag	pans window
Ctrl-Option-drag	zooms window
+/= (by the Delete key)	zooms in and out
Option-drag on numbed axis	pans only in that direction
Drag on numbered axis	scales that direction
S	syncs time to current keyframe
T	toggles time code/frame display
Shift-drag	selects keys
Ctrl-drag	deselects keys

Keyboard Shortcuts (continued)

Curve Editor

Cmd-A	selects all curves
Shift-A	selects all knots on active curve
Ctrl-click on tangent	breaks tangent
Shift-click on tangent	rejoins broken tangents
Q	moves selected points
W	scales points; this is a two-step process: you first click on the scale center, and then a second point to pull towards or away from the first point you clicked
X/Y	allows movement on only the X or Y axis; pressing them again frees that axis
H	flattens the tangents of a Hermite curve
V	toggles visibility of the selected curves
K	inserts a key on the current cursor position on the curve
Del	deletes active keys
Delete	removes curves from Editor (does not delete them)
F, Ctrl-F	frames selected curves
Shift-F	frames selected knots
Home	frames all curves

12

Lesson Files   Lessons > Lesson12 folder

Media   fairy.1-50.iff

fairy_bgd.1-50.iff

fairy_comp.1-50.iff

flicker.1-75.iff

Time   approximately 45 minutes

Goals   Use the FileIn node to blend frames

Apply the RBlur (radial blur) effect

See how SetDOD speeds up your processing

Change the length and position of a clip with TimeView

Animate with local variables and expressions

Transfer the animation of other nodes with parameter linking

Lesson **12**

Animation

In this module, you will take some computer-generated elements and create a finished element using advanced animation techniques such as parameter linking, local variables, and expressions. Animation is traditionally known as creating imagery on a frame-by-frame basis either by hand or digitally with computers. In this lesson, you will be using tools and techniques that will save the labor of ani-

This is the final animation you will create in this lesson.

Creating the Fairy

For this lesson, you will first create a fairy element and then add a soft flickering light to it.

FileIn and View the Source Clips

1   Start Shake.

2   FileIn the four elements from the Lesson12 folder using Cmd-A and select OK.

The clips are **fairy**, **fairy_bgd**, **flicker**, and **fairy_comp**.

3   Double-click on **fairy_comp** to see it in the Viewer.

4   Set the Globals timeRange to 1-50 and then click the Home icon at the bottom right of the interface to set the Time Bar to the same range.

5   Click the Flipbook icon and play the clip once it is loaded.

This is the final effect that you are going to build.

6 Close the flipbook.

7 Delete the **fairy_comp** clip from the Node workspace.

8 Make a flipbook of the **fairy** clip.

This is your fairy element.

9 Make a flipbook of the **fairy_bgd** clip.

This will serve as the background for the fairy element.

10 Close the flipbooks when you are done.

Using the FileIn Node to Blend Frames

The 3D artists spent all their time adding detail to the fairy, and the director decides that it doesn't feel right. He wants a softer, less defined look. Oh, well, back to the drawing board. To start with, you'll modify some of the Timing parameters located inside the fairy FileIn node. The Timing section of the FileIn node can take several frames and expand or contract them into a different frame range. Multiple frames will be blended together to give you a kind of motion blurred effect.

1 Double-click on the fairy FileIn node and click on the Timing tab within the Parameters workspace.

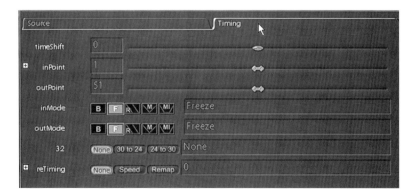

Normally, you might use the FileIn reTiming parameters to change the timing of a clip and add a bit of frame blending to smooth out the result. In this case, the length of the clip is good and just some frame blending should be added.

2 Change the reTiming mode from None to Speed.

Once you click on the Speed button, the reTiming menu opens up.

3 Set the range parameter to a value of 4.

Range controls how many frames beyond the normal averaging should be considered. For example, if you have a source clip of 20 frames and you want to extend it to 40 frames, each source frame would be considered in 2 output frames with a range setting of 1. With a range of 2, it would be considered in 4 output frames, giving you more blending. In this case, since you aren't changing the length of the clip, a range of 4 would blend 4 frames.

4 Make a flipbook of the **fairy** clip.

The **fairy** clip is now smoothed out as a result of the frame blending, giving it a softer look.

5 Close the flipbook.

Using SetDOD

In a moment, you will be using RBlur or Radial Blur to create a flare effect on the fairy element. This can be a time-intensive filter—using the SetDOD function will help speed things up. SetDOD limits the active area, or Domain of Definition, to a limited window. If you have an element that has a lot of black pixels around it, you can place a SetDOD node to isolate your area of interest, speeding up all processes on that image.

The fairy is a bit large, so you can scale it down.

1 Select the **fairy** clip and click on Move2D in the Transform tab.

2 Set the xScale to .5.

The yScale automatically sets itself to the same value as the xScale as a result of Shake's default parameter linking. This is good because it saves you time.

3 Add a SetDOD node from the Transform tab after Move2D1.

4 Set the left, right, top, and bottom sliders so that the bounding box is around the edges of the fairy image. The exact values are left=123, right=377, bottom=123, and top=377.

Filters added after this SetDOD will be limited to this smaller area of the screen, which will speed up rendering.

Add RBlur to the Fairies

RBlur blurs the image radially from a center point, creating flare effects. Adding an RBlur to the **fairy** clip will soften the fairy, making it less distinct. In fact, you will add two RBlurs and then combine them.

1 Add an RBlur from the Filter tab after SetDOD1.

2   Set the amplitude, which controls the amount of blur, to .25 and the quality to 1 (the highest setting).

3   Highlight SetDOD1, right-click on RBlur from the Filter tab, and choose Branch.

Another RBlur is created and branches off of SetDOD1.

4   Set the amplitude to .3 and the quality to 1.

5   Double-click on RBlur1 and then on RBlur2 to see the difference
between them.

The difference is slight, but they are different.

6   Select RBlur1 and choose Screen from the Layer tab.

The Screen function mimics the effect of exposing two film negatives
together and preserves the highlights.

7   Connect the output of RBlur2 to the second output of Screen1.

8 Make a flipbook of what you've done so far.

9 Play the flipbook and close it when you are done.

Isn't it pretty?

Adding Flicker

1 Make a flipbook of the **flicker** clip.

This is your flicker element.

2   Close the flipbook when you are done.

3   Select Screen1 and choose Screen from the Layer tab.

    Another Screen node is added after Screen1.

4   Connect **flicker** to the second output of Screen2.

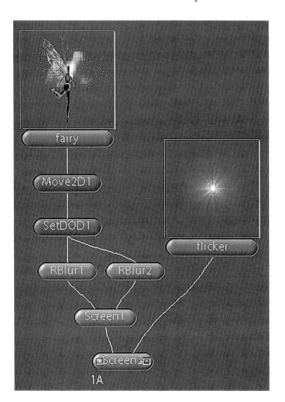

5   Make a flipbook of your composite and play what you have so far.

The flicker element is a bit harsh, and its timing could be adjusted relative to the fairy.

6   Close the flipbook when you are done.

Adjust Clip Timing with TimeView

If you want to move your clips or nodes relative to each other, you can do so in the TimeView.

1   Click on the TimeView tab located at the right of the Tool tabs window.

It will pop up showing you the clip length of your nodes.

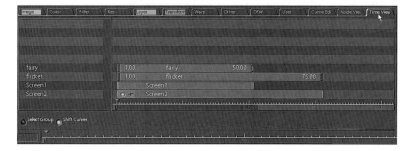

On the left side, you see a list of your elements.

Can you see that the **flicker** clip is 75 frames long? You need only 50 for the composite, so you can trim it down.

2   Grab the right edge of the **flicker** clip and drag it in to frame 65.

The clip length is shortened.

3   Drag the left edge of the clip to frame 5.

4   Open up **flicker**'s FileIn parameters by clicking on **flicker**'s parameter icon in the TimeView.

5   Look at the Parameters workspace.

The firstFrame/lastFrame parameters have been updated to reflect that you have trimmed the **flicker** clip at the head and tail.

6   Drag on the center of the **flicker** clip in the TimeView and drag it until it starts at frame 1.

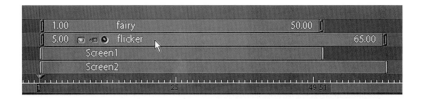

7   Take a look at the Timing tab in the Parameters workspace.

flicker's FileIn parameters now look like this:

Frames 5 to 65 of the original clip are positioned in the composite at frames 1 to 62.

NOTE ▶ When the Shift Curves option is turned on in the TimeView and you have any animated curves associated with the node you are moving, then those curves will also be repositioned.

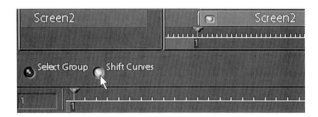

Create a Soft Flickering Light

You are going to take the harsh, flicker element and turn it into a nice, soft, flickering light.

1   Between **flicker** and Screen2, add a Blur node from the Filter tab and then a Brightness node from the Color tab.

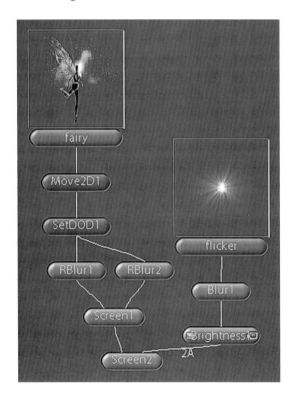

You can, of course, turn on Autokey and manually animate the brightness and blur parameters to create a soft flickering light, but that might strain your mouse finger. Instead, you will insert an expression into Brightness1's value parameter.

2   Double-click the Brightness1 node to make sure that you are viewing and editing its parameters.

3   Click in the value text field and replace the number 1 with the word *time*.

This takes the current frame number and uses it for the value parameter.

4   Move the Time Bar to various frames.

This, of course, brightens the image as you get to higher frames, since at frame 50 it creates a brightness value of 50.

5   Click on the + sign next to the value parameter.

You will see an expanded text field with your expression in it, time. The normal text field shows you the result of that expression at that frame. You can put any expression here, so do something clever like using a random function.

6   Type in *rnd(time)*.

This will return a random value between 0 and 1, with time as your variable. The rnd function isn't truly random, but by using time as your variable, you guarantee that the values will differ from frame to frame.

7   Click the Flipbook icon to preview the animation.

So far, you've added random flicker to an already flickering element.

8   Close the flipbook when you're done.

> **NOTE** ▶ If you move the slider on the value parameter by mistake, you will remove the expression. Simply retype the expression, or click Undo to get it back. The only exception to this behavior is if your expression is an animated curve that you create with keyframes.

9   To see the animated values in the Curve Editor, click on the clock icon next to value and open up the Curve Editor.

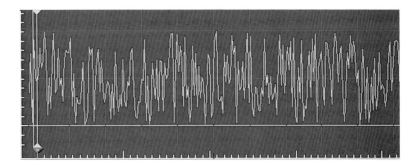

Your dreams of impressing those around you will no doubt be destroyed when you try clicking on the erratic curve. Nothing happens, because you aren't using keyframe animation. So, read on to see how you control an expression.

10 Right-click on Brightness1's Parameter1 tab. On the pop-up menu, select Create Local Variable.

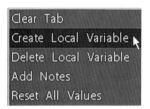

This means you will be adding an extra parameter to Brightness1 with which you can do whatever you want. A window will appear prompting you to name your local variable and select what type of variable it is:

▶ **float**
A number with a decimal place (.1, .5, 1.0, and so on)

▶ **int**
A rounded number (0, 1, 2, and so on)

▶ **string**
Characters ("Four score and twenty years ago…")

11 In the Variable name field, type *rndVal*, keep it on float, and click OK.

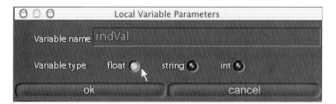

A new subtree named localParameters will appear in Brightness1's parameters.

If you adjust the slider, you will see that absolutely nothing happens.
Patience. First add another local variable and additional expressions.

12 Right-click again in the Parameter1 tab and select Create Local Variable.

13 Name it *animVal* and keep it on float.

It would be pretty impressive if you could set some keyframes in the
animVal local variable that would control the random time animation. Give it a try.

14 Go to frame 1 and turn on the Autokey for animVal, and enter three
keyframes. Enter values of .5 at frame 1, 2 at frame 20, and 1.5 at frame 50.

15 Place your cursor over the Curve Editor and press the Home key on
the keyboard to show all of your curves.

This centers all of your curves within the Curve Editor, but the
animVal keyframes are not controlling the random time animation.
To do this, you first have to move the rnd(time) expression from value
to rndVal and then write a new expression for value.

16 Click on the word "value" (a little hand holding a piece of paper should
appear), drag down to rndVal, and release the mouse button.

17 Open up rndVal's subtree.

You should see rnd(time) as its new expression.

18 Open up value's subtree, double-click on value's expression, and replace it with *rndVal*anim Val.*

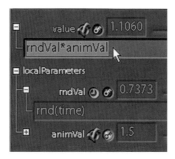

This will multiply the results of rndVal and animVal together.

19 Make sure value and animVal, but not rndVal, are loaded in the Curve Editor.

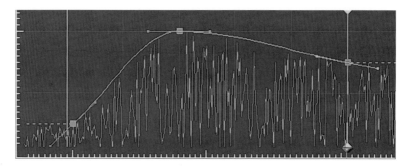

Finally, you can see that the curve is modifying the shape of the otherwise random curve.

20 Go ahead and grab the keyframes or insert a new one, and you change the form of the random shape.

21 Drag the Time Bar to various frames to get an idea of what the animation looks like.

Now that you can control the random flickering, you can link the animation in Brightness1's value parameter to Blur1's xPixels. This will give the blur the same random animation as in Brightness1's value parameter.

22 Click on the right side of the Blur1 node to edit its parameters.

23 Click in the xPixels text field and type *Brightness1.value*75*.

The *75 is for multiplying the result of Brightness1's value animation, which is only in a range of 0.5 to 2. Multiplying by 75 makes the effect of the blur noticeable.

24 Drag the Time Bar again to see what is happening.

The blur randomly animates along with the flickering light through parameter linking. The last step will be to combine the random flicker animation with the original flicker element.

25 Select **flicker** and right-click on Screen from the Layer tab and choose branch.

26 Connect the output of Brightness1 into the second input of Screen3 and take the output of Screen3 and put it into the second input of Screen2.

Your tree should look like this:

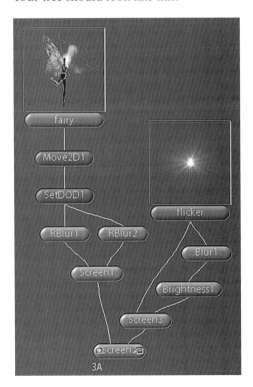

27 Double-click on the Screen2 node, make a flipbook, and play it.

The fairy is now complete and ready to be placed over the background.

28 Close your flipbook.

Add the Fairy to the Background

1 Add a Screen node from the Layer tab after Screen2.

2 Attach the output of the **fairy_bgd** clip into the second input of Screen4.

The fairy is a bit big compared to the resolution of the **fairy_bgd** clip and could use some animation to make it fly. You can create your own animation of the fairy flying by creating a Move2D node animation after the Screen2 node, but I have already created one for you. If you want to create your own animation, you can skip steps 3–5, but you'll need to add a Move2D node between Screen2 and Screen 4 and animate it.

3 Select File > Add Script.

4 Go to the Lesson12/scripts folder, select **Move2D_fairy.shk**, and click OK.

A single node called Move2D_fairy is loaded into the Node workspace.

5 Insert the Move2D_fairy node between Screen2 and Screen4.

6   Double-click on the Screen4 node, make a flipbook, and play it.

Not too bad. The fairy flies from right to left across the screen and rests in front of one of the windows. To make it look like a real flying fairy, it should have some random movement to it. You can accomplish this by adding a CameraShake node.

The CameraShake node applies noise functions onto the Pan values, resulting in what looks like, you guessed it, camera shake.

7   Close your flipbook.

8   Insert a CameraShake node from the Transform tab after Move2D_fairy.

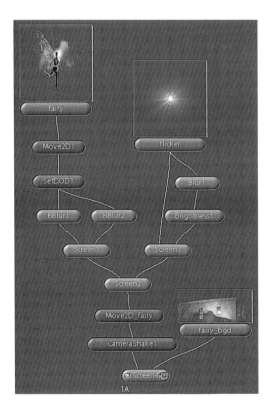

9   Go to frame 1, turn on the keyframe parameter for the xFrequency, and set a value of .5.

The yFrequency will automatically follow the animation of xFrequency because of Shake's default parameter linking.

10   Go to frame 30 and set the xFrequency to a value of .25.

Animating the xFrequency will give some randomness to the already random camera shake.

11   Double-click on the Screen4 node, make a flipbook, and play it.

It's a thing of beauty.

12   Close your flipbook and quit Shake.

What You've Learned

- The Timing section of the FileIn node can take several frames and expand or contract them into a different frame range.

- SetDOD limits the active area, or Domain of Definition, to a limited window. If you have an element that has a lot of black pixels around it, you can place a SetDOD node to isolate your area of interest, speeding up all processes on that image.

- A local variable is a variable that is specific to a node.

13

Lesson Files
Media

Time

approximately 1 hour and 30 minutes

Goals

Track multiple points

Offset track points

Average multiple tracks

Perform a four-point track using Stabilize

Lesson 13
Tracking

Tracking is a technique that involves selecting a particular region of an image and analyzing its motion over time. Once analyzed, the motion can be applied to another clip.

In this lesson you will add a four-point track to this wristwatch and add the composite of the animated watch face.

One-Point Tracking

As mentioned in chapter 11, Shake has three tracking nodes: Tracker, Stabilize, and MatchMove. Tracker is a generic generator of an unlimited amount of curves and is useful for passing these curves to the transform nodes. Stabilize removes bounce or jitter from a clip and can generate up to four trackers to be used in position, scaling, and/or rotational stabilization. MatchMove can track up to four points and apply the tracked motion of one clip to another. To refresh your memory about the tracking workflow and how to create a tracking curve, re-read pages 285 to 287.

Despite all of the demos you love to see, tracking is rarely a magic bullet that works on the first attempt. In the MatchMove exercise, I'll provide you with some strategies to help you get accurate tracks. MatchMove can track up to four points and apply the tracked motion of one clip to another.

View the Clips

It is always best to view the clips that you'll be tracking. It will help in choosing the proper feature to track.

1   Start Shake.

2   Use Cmd-A to FileIn all the files from the Lesson13/building folder and click OK.

   You should have three clips: **building**, **building_comp**, and **neon_globe**.

3   Start by setting the Global timeRange to 1-50.

4   While you're at it, click the Home icon at the bottom right of the screen to make the Time Bar low and high values match the Globals timeRange.

5   Make a flipbook of **building_comp**.

The globe was tracked and composited on top of the building.

6   Make a flipbook of your two elements: **building** and **neon_globe**.

You will be motion tracking the **building** clip and applying that motion to the **neon_globe** clip.

7   Close all your flipbooks when you're done.

Pick a Good Reference Pattern

The ideal pattern is one that doesn't change perspective, scale, or rotation, and does not go offscreen or get obscured by other objects. It also doesn't change overall brightness or color, is very high contrast, and is distinct from other patterns in the same neighborhood. Meanwhile, in the real world, you have to contend with all of these factors, which will cause your tracker or trackers to lose accuracy. A successful composite requires an accurate track.

1   Go to the Transform tab, right-click on MatchMove, and select Create.

2 Connect the output of the **building** clip to the right input (background input) of MatchMove1.

3 Position the tracker over the 12 o'clock position.

You might want to zoom in for precise placement of the tracker.

4 Size the reference pattern so that it has only a few pixels around 12 o'clock.

Pick a Good Search Region

You should position and size your search region to match both the movement and the patterns near your reference pattern. Set it to the maximum amount your track point will move between frames. The larger this is, the slower the tracker will be.

Size the search region around the outside of the crosshairs.

How do you know if the search region is the right size? If you make the search region too small, the tracker will lose the reference pattern. If it's unnecessarily large, it will take too long to process. The key is to make the search region as small as possible without getting tracking errors.

Identify the Channel with the Highest Contrast

- The tracker works best with a high-contrast reference pattern. To the human eye, you see contrast as represented by value. However, you may sometimes have higher contrast in saturation or hue, so switch over to a different color space with the matchSpace parameter located in the tolerances parameter group. In this case with the building, luminance is fine.

- A shot may also have a higher contrast in a specific RGB channel than in the others; for example, the blue channel might have a bigger range than the red or green. In that case, you could put a Reorder node (from the Color tab) with the channels set to bbb on the image, and then track with luminance as your matchSpace.

Track the Image in Its Highest Quality

- Ideally, you should be tracking an image with the most amount of raw data, so turn off both proxyScale and proxyRatio settings. Once the tracks are done, return to your proxy settings.

- In some cases, you may in fact want to modify your images to improve contrast in the reference pattern, either with a ContrastLum or ContrastRGB. Since you are just using this image to generate tracks, you are not obliged to keep the contrast-modified image for the rest of your composite.

- Finally, sometimes you may be having problems with random film grain being too severe, and your reference pattern becomes useless. Activate the preProcess button in the Tracker before you track to reduce the effects of grain.

Track the Building

Enough talking already, it's time for some tracking.

1   Turn limitProcessing on in the MatchMove1 node.

This will speed up processing. You'll see what I mean in a moment.

2   Click on the forward tracking button.

The Track buttons are located under the Viewer when your tracking node is loaded into the Parameters workspace.

The screen turns black except for the area enclosed within the search region because limitProcessing is turned on. This will create a Domain of Definition (DOD) around the bounding box of all active trackers. Only that portion of the image will be loaded from disk when tracking, therefore it will go more quickly. This has no effect on the final output image.

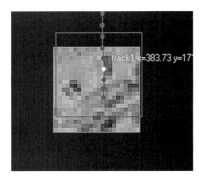

MatchMove tracks each frame of the **building** clip and superimposes the tracked points for each frame.

Now that you have acquired the tracking data, you can apply it to another clip.

3   Connect the output of **neon_globe** into the foreground or first input of MatchMove1.

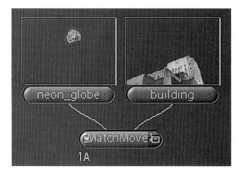

4　In the outputType pop-up box, select IAdd.

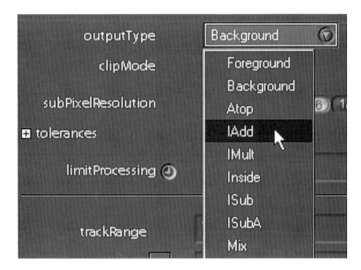

This selects the method by which you will combine the foreground
with the background.

5　Check that 1 pt is selected as the trackType.

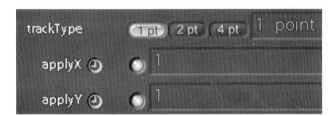

trackType allows you to choose what type of transformation you
want, either 1 pt (panning), 2 pt (panning, scaling, and/or rotation),
or 4 pt (cornerpinning) stabilization. 1 pt is the default.

6　Turn on applyTransform.

The tracking data is now applied to the **neon_globe** clip.

7   Drag the Time Bar to various frames.

The globe's motion is now following the motion of the **building** clip. It's not in the right position, but it is tracked.

8   Go to frame 1, highlight the **neon_globe** clip, and select Move2D from the Transform tab.

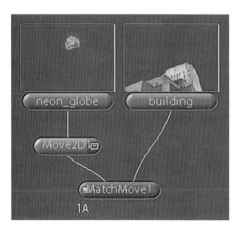

9   Reposition the neon_globe with Move_2D1 so that it rests on the top of the building.

10   Double-click on MatchMove1 and click the Flipbook icon under the Viewer to test the results of your track.

The track looks pretty good, but what if your reference pattern became obscured at a certain point?

Offset Tracking

Sometimes your original reference pattern gets obscured. In these instances, you can offset the search region from the track point. You will simulate this with a new track and the **building** clip.

1   Turn off applyTransform so that MatchMove1 is not trying to move the foreground at the same time as you are trying to track.

2   Set the outputType pop-up to Background so that the foreground is not composited with the background.

3   Scroll down the Parameters workspace and turn off the Visibility of track1 and turn on the Visibility of track2.

4   Go to frame 50.

Just for fun, you will track track2 backwards.

5   Position track2 over the 6 o'clock position of the clock and size the reference pattern and search region as you did for track1.

6 Click on the reverse tracking button and press the Esc key at about frame 25 to stop the track.

7 Drag the Time Bar to frame 25 if you are not already there.

The track point at frame 25 just became obscured. You're pretending, remember. If you turn on the Offset Track function, the search region and reference pattern can be moved to a new location while keeping the track point in the same location.

▶ **Offset Track Off**
The track search region/reference pattern and the track point are linked. If you move one, the other follows.

▶ **Offset Track On**
The search region/reference pattern and the track point are offset from each other.

8 Turn on Offset tracking.

Make sure to turn on Offset tracking before you move the search region.

9   Position track2's search region and reference pattern over the 11 o'clock position.

10   Click on the reverse tracking button to continue tracking.

The track point follows the same path, but the new search region is used to acquire the tracking data.

Averaging Tracks

A common technique is to track forward from the first frame to the last, and then create a second track, tracking backward from the last frame to the first. It just so happens that you have already done this. What a coincidence. These two tracks are then averaged together to hopefully derive a more accurate track. Since MatchMove always uses track1 for x/y transformations, you will need to copy track1 to a different track before averaging.

1   At the bottom of the Parameters workspace, right-click on track3 and select Load Track.

2   When the Select Track menu pops up, choose MatchMove.track1 and
     click OK.

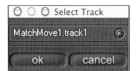

track1 is loaded into track3.

3   Right-click on track1 and select Average Tracks.

This will pop up a window giving you up to four input trackers to
average together.

4   Select MatchMove1.track2 and MatchMove1.track3 in the first two pop-ups, leaving the last two at none. Click OK when you're done.

This works by creating an expression in both the track1X and track1Y parameters. The expression for the 1X parameter looks like this:

(MatchMove1.track3X + MatchMove1.track2X) / 2

You can see the effect of the Average clearly in the Curve Editor.

5   Expand the track1, track2, and track3 subtrees and click on the clock icon next to the trackX parameter for each track.

6 Select the Curve Editor in the Tool tabs.

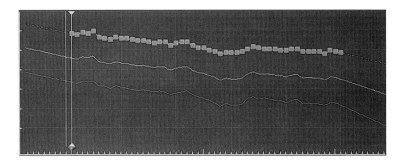

The center curve represents the averaged track1. Slight differences in the tracks have been averaged together, yielding a more accurate result. Let's take a look.

7 Select IAdd from the outputType pop-up box.

8 Turn on applyTransform.

9 Click the Flipbook icon and play it when it's done loading.

You should have a pretty decent track at this point.

10 Save your script.

Four-Point Tracking

Four-point tracking is traditionally used to match the perspective of one shot and apply it to another—for instance, tracking the four corners of a sign and replacing it with a new billboard. In this example, you will be tracking a wristwatch and placing a fancy animated element inside of it.

For this exercise, you will be using Stabilize instead of MatchMove. This has several advantages:

- More flexibility in what extra nodes you can apply because you separate the composite out of MatchMove.
- Better control over transform concatenation of the foreground.
- Better control over premultiplication of the foreground.
- Accurate pass-through of On-Screen controls.
- Intuitive control of foreground positioning.

Workflow for Matchmoving with Stabilize

- Attach Stabilize to the node you are going to be tracking and generate your tracks—in this example, the watch.
- Extract the node (select and press the E key), and re-attach it to the image you want to transform—in this example, the graphic.
- Turn on the transformation with applyTransform and change Stabilize to match.
- Composite the Stabilize over the background with an Over node.
- Insert a Viewport node above the Stabilize to adjust the frame around what you want to track.
- Insert a CornerPin between the Viewport and the Stabilize. This is used to match the foreground clip's perspective and size to the background image

Viewing the Elements

1　Choose File > New Script and answer No when prompted to save.

2 Use Cmd-A to FileIn all the files from the Lesson13/watch folder and click OK.

You should have six clips: **watch**, **watch_comp**, **graphic**, **graphic_mask**, **highlight**, and **highlight_mask**.

3 Start by setting the Global timeRange to 1–50.

4 While you're at it, click the Home key at the bottom right of the screen to make the Time Bar low and high values match the Globals timeRange.

5 Make a flipbook of the **watch_comp** clip.

A four-point track was used to match the perspective of the watch and place the animated graphic inside.

6 Make a flipbook of your two sequences: **watch** and **graphic**.

The **watch** clip has four points on it, obviously placed by a visual effects supervisor who cares. This will make tracking relatively painless. The **graphic** clip is a nicely animated element that will be used for the foreground insert.

7   Close all your flipbooks.

8   Look at the **highlight** clip in the Viewer.

This is a premade highlight texture that will be used to place a highlight over the tracked graphic. There are also two premade masks that will be used to mask the foreground graphic and highlight elements.

Take a look at the premade masks.

9   View the alpha channel in the Viewer.

10 First, double-click on the **graphic_mask** clip and then on the **highlight_mask** clip.

These are the masks you will be using.

11 Set the Viewer to view the RGB channels by pressing the C key.

Track the Watch

Start off by tracking the watch with a Stabilize node.

ıt the **watch** clip and select a Stabilize node from the
m tab.

At frame 1 of the sequence, you will place four tracks starting at the lower-left corner and moving counter-clockwise.

2   Go to frame 1 of the sequence.

3   Place track1 over the lower-left dot of the watch.

4   Set the subPixelResolution to a value of ¹⁄₆₄.

You need to make sure the elements fit together seamlessly, so the most accurate setting will be used.

5   Turn on the visibility for track2 through track4 at the bottom of the Parameter window.

6 Place track2 on the lower-right dot, track3 on the upper-right dot, and track4 on the upper-left dot.

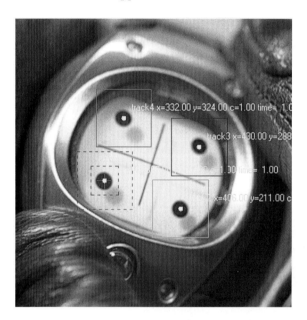

7 Turn limitProcessing on, which will make the tracking analysis go faster.

8 Click on the forward tracking button.

The screen turns black except for the area around the four tracks because limitProcessing is active and the motion of the **watch** clip is analyzed.

Applying the Tracking Data

Now that the motion of the watch is analyzed, the data can be applied to the graphic.

1   Go back to frame 1.

2   With the cursor over the Node workspace, select the Stabilize1 node and press the E key to extract it.

3   Connect the **graphic** clip into the Stabilize1 node.

4   Insert an Over node from the Layer tab after Stabilize1 and connect the **watch** clip into the right input of Over1.

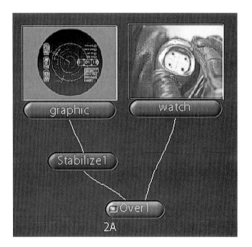

5   Turn on preMultiply in the Over1 node.

The graphic is composited over the watch, but the tracking data needs to be activated in the Stabilize node.

6   Click on the right side of Stabilize1 to edit its parameters.

7 In Stabilize1, make applyTansform active, set inverseTransform to match, and click on 4 pt for the trackType.

8 Drag through the Time Bar.

The tracking data is applied, but the graphic should be positioned with a Viewport and CornerPin.

9 Go back to frame 1.

10 Highlight the **graphic** clip and select a Viewport node from the Transform tab.

Viewport is like a Crop, but it keeps the image information outside of the frame so you can do transformations afterwards. Using a Viewport will help you to better place the **graphic** clip in conjunction with the CornerPin node that will be added in a moment.

11 View and Edit Viewport1.

12 Adjust the edges of the Viewport1 node to the edges of the circle around the graphic.

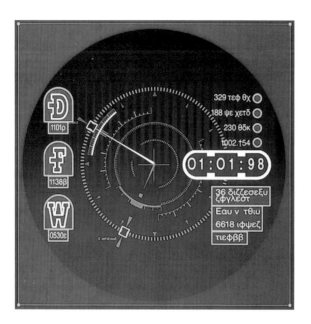

13 Add a CornerPin node after Viewport1 and click on the left side of Over1 to view the composite.

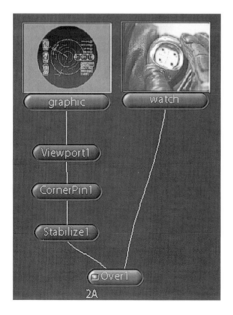

14 Place the four corners of the CornerPin into the center of the four dots on the watch. Changing the points in the Viewer will change the x0, y0 through x3, y3 parameter values.

The CornerPin node puts the graphic into the same perspective as the watch.

15 Click and drag halfway between the points of the corner pin on the top, bottom, left, and right sides to size the graphic, which has to cover the entire face of the watch. This offsets the points in the corner pin but keeps the points in proper perspective.

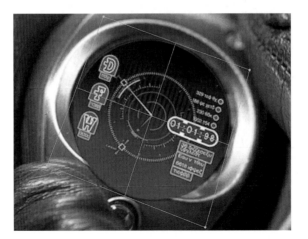

16 Click on the Flipbook icon to see what has been done so far.

The shot seems to be tracked pretty well. Now for the final touches.

17 Close the flipbook when you are finished viewing.

Masking the Graphic

The graphic is sized properly, but it should be masked to the face of the watch.

1 Insert an Inside node from the Layer tab after the **graphic** clip.

The Inside node places one image within the area of a mask from another image.

2 Plug the **graphic_mask** clip into the second input of the Inside1 node.

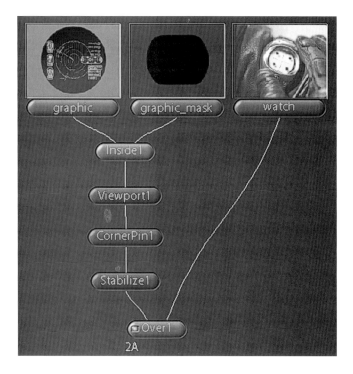

The graphic is masked to the outline of the watch face.

3   Click on the right side of CornerPin1 to edit its parameters and fine-tune the four corners so that the graphic fits exactly into the face of the watch.

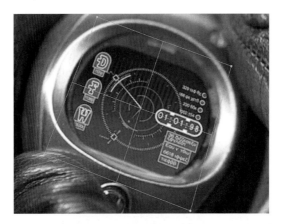

Color Correcting the Watch

The edge around the graphic would look better if it were a bit darker, giving it the illusion that it is set into the face of the watch. You can achieve this with a little bit of color correction.

1   Add a Mult node from the Color tab after the **watch** clip.

2   Plug the output of Stabilize1 into the mask input of Mult1.

    By using the mask of Stabilize1, you can limit the color correction to the watch face.

3   View and edit the Mult1 node.

4   Press the V key (adjusts value or brightness) and drag over the Color box to a value of .5.

The brightness has been cut in half, but it looks as if the matte could be dilated a touch.

5 Insert a DilateErode node from the Filter tab between Stabilize1 and the mask input of Mult1.

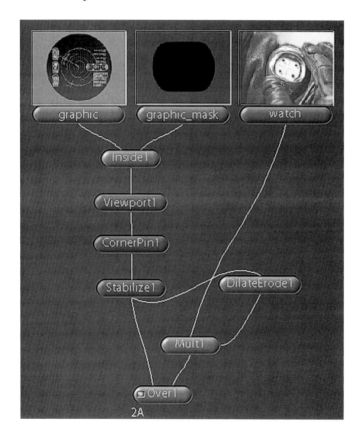

6 While viewing the Mult1 node, edit DilateErode1 so that the xPixel and yPixel values equal 1.5.

7 View the Over1 node.

At this point, the graphic has a realistic border around it.

8   Make a flipbook to see your progress and close it when you are done.

Adding the Highlight

The last step to finishing this composite is to add a highlight over the face of the watch.

1   Copy and paste Viewport1, CornerPin1, and Stabilize1 so that the **highlight** clip will have the same motion as the graphic and watch.

2   Connect the **highlight** clip into Viewport2.

3   Create a Color node from the Image tab and set its resolution to 720 × 540.

    The Color node will be used to take the color of the watch and apply it to the highlight.

4   Highlight Over1 and select a KeyMix from the Layer tab.

5   Hook up Color1 to the middle input and Stabilize2 to the far right input of KeyMix1.

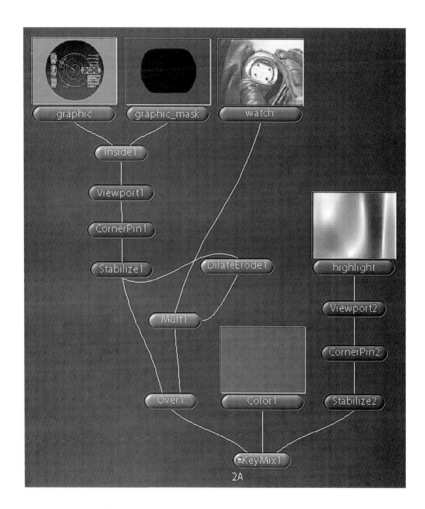

2A

Since KeyMix1's channel parameter is looking for an alpha channel to composite the Color1 node over the watch, you should change the channel parameter. This is because the **highlight** clip has no alpha channel.

6 Set the channel parameter of KeyMix1 to G.

You have achieved reflection. It's the wrong color, but a reflection nonetheless.

7 Edit the Color node and click on the Color Picker next to the Color parameter.

8 Click on the blue metal at the top of the watch.

All that's left is to use the **highlight_mask** to mask off the highlight.

9 Click on the Node View tab so you can see your tree.

10 Add an Inside function after the highlight node and connect the **highlight_mask** into the right input.

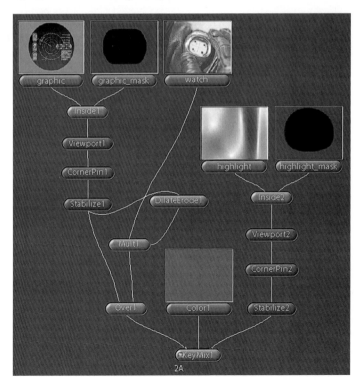

11 Double-click on the KeyMix1 node and set the Opacity to 65.

12 Make a flipbook.

Now, that is how you do a four-point track.

13 Quit Shake.

Tracker Adjustments

If the tracker misses, which it never does, you have a few options:

- Stop the tracker, go to the bad frame and reposition the tracking cross, and click the tracking button again. You don't need to go back to your start frame. Frames that are not within the tolerance (see below) are marked in red on the Time Bar.

- Activate the preprocess flag in the tracker. This applies a small blur to the footage to reduce irregularities due to film grain.

- Lower your referenceTolerance value, and track again from the beginning or from the frame before the bad frames. The lower the reference-Tolerance, the more forgiving the tracker will be—but it will also be less accurate. Access the referenceTolerance parameter by clicking on the + next to the tolerances parameter group in your tracking node.

- Start over, and switch referenceBehavior, located in the tolerances parameter group, from use start frame to update every frame. This means that instead of trying to compare the tracking region with the first "pure" frame, it will try to match to the previous frame. If you retrack from the middle of a sequence, it will consider your new start frame as your reference frame with either setting.

- At any time, you can turn on the Autokey button in the Viewer and manually adjust a tracking point by simply grabbing it and putting it where you need to. You can use the + and − keys by the Backspace key to zoom in and out to see the points easier.

- Change the matchSpace from luminance to hue or saturation and retrack. The matchSpace parameter determines which image value the tracking algorithm will be using. The matchSpace controls are in the tolerances parameter group of your tracking node. Just click on the + next to tolerances to reveal the matchSpace parameters.

- Change the subPixelResolution to a lower value to get more precise tracks. The tracker will take longer, but it will be more accurate.

NOTE ▶ When checking the accuracy of your tracks, it's best to turn off applyTransform to see if the curves are matching up to the points.

• Another technique you can use to assist with difficult shots is to manually insert tracking keyframes. For example, if you have 100 frames to track, you can put in a keyframe every 5 or 10 frames with the Autokey feature. A helpful trick is to set an increment of 5 or 10 in the Time Bar and press the left arrow or right arrow to jump by the increment amount and set keyframes. Once your keyframes are manually entered, return to frame 1 and set the failureBehavior under the tolerances submenu to "use existing key to predict location." The tracker searches along the tracker's pre-existing motion path to find matching patterns.

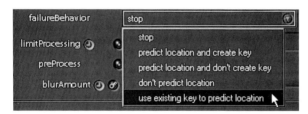

What You've Learned

• Shake has three tracking nodes: Tracker, Stabilize, and MatchMove.

• The reference pattern defines a small pattern that will be searched for in subsequent frames; the search region is the maximum amount your tracking point will move between frames.

• The tracker works best with a high-contrast reference pattern.

• The Average tracks function enables you to combine multiple tracks.

• Offset Tracking is used when your reference pattern becomes obscured. In this mode, the track point follows the same path, but a new search region/reference pattern is used to acquire the tracking data.

14

Lesson Files

Time

Goals

approximately 1 hour

Use command-line Shake in the Terminal window

Load single images and sequences into a flipbook

Compare images

Convert files

Get help

Get image information

Execute command-line compositing

Lesson **14**

Command Line

This lesson shows you how to use Shake in the OS X Terminal program to launch flipbooks, do file conversions, launch scripts, and generally execute any string of commands that are also available in the interface. I highly encourage you to learn the command-line syntax, because it's often much easier to do things without firing up the interface.

You can use the command line to composite clips efficiently in Shake without launching the interface.

Shake in the Command Line

Every function that you can perform in the interface can also be executed in a Terminal window, usually in what is known as a shell. The command line is perfect for when you know exactly (or almost exactly) what you want to do, and it's not very complicated. Its great benefit is speed. If you just want to take high-resolution images and make video-resolution copies with a change in color, typing that out may be easier than actually launching the interface and connecting all of the nodes.

Common Command-Line Uses

- Resize, rotate, crop, or flip/flop images from scans
- Add sharpening filters as you resize elements upwards
- Change image file formats
- Place the luminance of an image into its alpha channel
- Load images into a flipbook for playback
- Render scripts
- Check a rendered, computer-generated element over a background plate
- Renumber and rename files
- Compare two images

Most importantly, you can also execute work while snugly in bed. When you remotely log in to your office in the middle of the night because someone forgot to copy some needed files, you'll really love that Shake has an expansive command-line feature set.

Some Useful Unix Commands

Unix (pronounced yoo-niks) is a popular, multiuser, multitasking operating system. Originally designed in the early 1970s by just a handful of programmers to be used only by programmers, Unix is known for its cryptic commands and general lack of user-friendliness.

Even though you would never know it, Mac OS X is based on Unix. You can run and execute Unix commands as well as Shake command-line functions in the OS X Terminal program. So, getting familiar with some of the more common Unix commands is a good idea. Here are a few that you'll find useful:

cd

> cd changes the current working directory to a new directory. If you don't specify anything after typing cd, you will change directories to your home directory.
>
> Usage: cd [*directory*]
>
> Options:
>
> ../ : Takes you up one directory.
>
> ../.. : Takes you up two directories.
>
> ../../..: Takes you up three directories. You get the idea.
>
> **NOTE ▶** In Unix, using correct syntax is important. For example, cd ..
> will take you up one directory level, but cd.. (no space) will return cd..:
> Command not found.

cp

> cp copies a file or files to a specified directory under the same name. If the destination file exists, it will be overwritten.
>
> Usage: cp *file1 file2* or cp -r *files directory*.
>
> Options:
>
> -r: Copies a directory and all of its contents.

ls

> ls lists the files contained in the current or specified directory.
>
> Usage: ls [*options*] [*directory*]

Options:

-a: Lists all files including "." or hidden files.

-l: Long format listing.

-lrt: Long format listing in reverse order by time. This is good for showing the last set of files recorded in a directory.

mv

mv moves a file or directory to a new name or location.

Usage: mv *file target*

rm

rm deletes one or more files.

Usage: rm [*options*] *files*

Options:

-r: removes a directory and all of its contents.

Loading a Single Image

Ready or not, let's use Shake in the command line.

1   Start the Terminal program located in the Applications/Utilities folder.

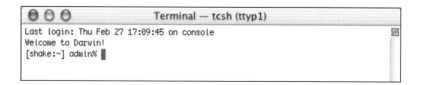

2   Navigate to the Lesson14 folder using the cd command. If you copied the Lessons folder directly into your Macintosh hard drive, type, *cd /Lessons/Lesson14* and press Enter.

NOTE ▶ You must press the Enter key on the keyboard to execute command-line functions.

Instead of typing out every letter of a file or folder, you can use the file-completion shortcut in the Terminal window: whenever you press the Tab key, it will list all potential files that match what you type.

3   Type *shake li* and then press the Tab key.

This will type out **lisa.iff** for you.

4   Press Enter.

The **lisa** clip is shown in a Viewer.

Image courtesy of Thinkstock.

You can see the image name and resolution in the title bar.

5   Drag the left mouse button over the image to see the x,y coordinates and the Red, Green, Blue, and Alpha values in the title bar.

Shake measures the image starting in the lower left corner at 0,0. This means that the right edge will be the width of the image minus one. The same goes for the top of the image.

Here are some of the things that you can do in the Viewer:

▶   Zoom in on the image with the – and = keys near the delete key.

▶   Pan the image using the right mouse button.

▶   Center the image and remove all zooming by pressing the Home key.

▶   View the Red, Green, Blue, and Alpha channels by pressing the R, G, B, or A keys. To go back to full color, press C.

▶   Close the image quickly by pressing Esc.

6   Close the **lisa.iff** flipbook.

NOTE ▶ When you are done with each command line, close the flipbook so you can move on to the next step.

To view more than one image, enter multiple filenames.

7   Type *shake lisa.iff bg.iff*.

Two flipbooks open up to show each image.

8   Close all of the flipbooks.

TIP ▶ You can repeat previous commands by using the up arrow on the command line. Each time you press it, it will list the previous command, stepping back through your history. Use the left and right arrows to change portions of the command. Pressing the down arrow will take you to the next command in your history list.

Loading a Sequence

Loading a sequence of images is just like loading a single image, except that you give a frame range and put in a marker in the input filename that represents where the frames are. The marker can handle unpadded or padded frame numbers (for example, image.1 or image.0001). If you want padded frames, use #. For unpadded frames, use @. You can also use printf-like formatting, such as %d, %04d, and so on. Finally, you may also use an arbitrary number of @ signs for padding other than four digits.

Here are some examples:

Shake Format	Reads/Writes
image.#.iff	image.0001.iff, image.0002.iff
image.%04d.iff	image.0001.iff, image.0002.iff
image.@.iff	image.1.iff, image.2.iff
image.%d.iff	image.1.iff, image.2.iff
image.@@@.iff	image.001.iff, image.002.iff
image.%3d.iff	image.001.iff, image.002.iff

1   To load up man.0001.iff through man.0014.iff, type
shake man.#.iff -t 1-14.

The –t flag in the command line stands for time and specifies the frame range of your sequence.

You should have 14 frames loaded in a flipbook.

2   To play the images, press . (the > key).

3   To play backwards, press , (the < key).

4   To stop playing, press the spacebar.

Here are some other things you can do with a flipbook:

▶   Step through the animation by pressing the left and right arrow keys.

▶   Scrub through the animation by pressing Shift and clicking the left mouse button.

▶   Ping-pong the playback by pressing Shift->.

▶   Play through once by pressing Ctrl->.

▶   Increase or decrease the frame rate by pressing the + or – keys on the numeric keypad.

NOTE ▶ The frame rate is displayed on the title bar. If you are getting real-time playback, it will say "Locked." Otherwise, it will drop down.

▶ Play back in real time by pressing the T key. This will drop frames if Shake can't maintain the desired speed. If Shake drops frames, it will tell you what percent is being dropped.

Using the -t option to describe your frame range is an extremely flexible way to look at any variety or order of images.

5   Type *shake man.#.iff -t 1-14x2*.

Only frames 1, 3, 5, 7, 9, 11, and 13 are loaded into the flipbook.

6   Step through the clip with the arrow keys.

On the title bar, observe how the name of the clip updates showing every other frame.

Comparing Images

You can load two images simultaneously into a flipbook to compare them.

1   Type *shake bg.iff -compare car.rla*.

2   To compare the images, press Shift-Ctrl-left mouse button and slide back and forth inside the flipbook.

You can also:

- ▶ Switch the compare buffers by pressing S.
- ▶ Toggle the vertical and horizontal splits by pressing V and H.
- ▶ Fade between the images by pressing F.

The cool thing is that the compare function works with moving images.

Converting Files

So far, you have been loading images into a flipbook. If you do not put an output file in the command line, this is what it will do. To convert an image to a different file, merely add an output filename following the –fileout command.

1 Type *shake lisa.iff -fileout fancy_girl.jpg*

or

2 Type *shake lisa.iff -fo fancy_girl.jpg*.

This writes **lisa.iff** as the JPEG image fancy_girl.jpg.

If you want to convert an entire sequence, use the -t flag.

3 Type *shake -v man.#.iff -fo man.@.rgb -t 1-10*.

This will write man.0001.iff as man.1.rgb, up to frame 10. The @ sign sits in as the unpadded frame number symbol. Since you used the -v (verbose) flag, Shake shows you how long each frame takes to render.

Shake never makes explicit changes to the data in an image based on the file format that is being used. Thus, there would be no automatic log-to-linear conversion if you were to convert from the Cineon file format. To make such a conversion, include a delogc command.

Getting Help

As you may suspect, there are a lot of Shake commands. These are a few methods (other than reading the Shake Reference Guide) for getting help in the command line. First of all, to figure out a command, you can type *shake -help command_name.*

1   Type *shake -help delogc*

In the Terminal window, Shake gives you the syntax for the delogc command:

-delogc [rOffset] [gOffset] [bOffset] [black] [white] [nGamma] [dGamma] [softclip]

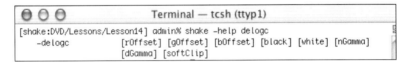

You can also get general help on a concept, such as multiplying.

2   Type *shake -help mul.*

Shake returns the following output in the Terminal window:

-imult

-mmult

-mult

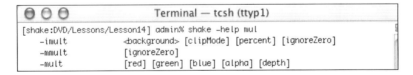

3   If you would like to see a complete list of commands, type *shake -help*.

This displays a list of every single Shake command, as well as any macros that you created.

```
  ● ● ●             Terminal — tcsh (ttyp1)
                    <conformKernel> <frameListFileName> <width> <height>
     -vtrin         [autoAlpha] [deInterlacing] [tcm] [in] [out] [duration]
                    [reel] [clip] [...]
     -vtrout        [tcm] [in] [out] [duration] [yuvEncode] [...]
     -vv
     -vwipe         [i2] [blur] [reverse] [mixPercent]
     -warpx         [oversamping] [xExpr] [yExpr] [xDelta] [yDelta]
     -window        [left] [bottom] [right] [top]
     -xor           <background> [clipMode] [useMatte]
     -yiqtorgb
     -yuvtorgb
     -z             <scale>
     -zblur         [amount] [near] [far] [focusCenter] [focusRange] [steps]
                    [stepBlend]
```

Getting Image Info

Shake can quickly get information about an image with the -info command. If you are using this option, it will not pop the image into a flipbook but instead will give you a text output in the Terminal window:

1   Type *shake lisa.iff -info*.

In the shell window, you'll see the following:

Filename: lisa.iff

Type: RGBA

Size: 480x720

Depth: 8 bits

Z-Buffer: none

Format: Shake

It gives you lots of info, which is pretty self-explanatory. If you change the parameters, the info command will reflect this.

2   Type *shake lisa.iff -zoom 2 -bytes 2 -reorder rgbn -info*.

In the shell window, you'll see the following:

Filename: lisa.iff

Type: RGB

Size: 960x1440

Depth: 16 bits

Z-Buffer: none

Format: Shake

I zoomed up the image with -zoom, which gives me my higher resolution. I also put in 2 bytes per channel, which gives me a bit depth of 16 bits, and I stripped out the alpha channel (n in the -reorder option means "no channel"), leaving a three-plane image. Shake doesn't process the image unless you use a –fileout command followed by an output image.

Basic Command-Line Compositing

Basic compositing on the command line can be very useful, especially for testing composites. Let's start by viewing the elements.

1   Type *shake bg.iff car.rla sign_mask.iff*.

Three flipbooks open. Look at each flipbook, and when you get to car.rla, look at its alpha channel, which we will use to composite the car over the background.

2   With car.rla's window active, press the A key to view the alpha channel.

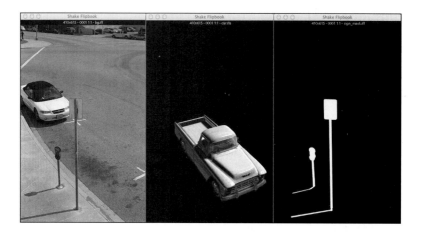

We want to place car.rla over bg.iff except in the white areas shown in the sign_mask.iff image.

3   Close all three flipbooks.

4   Type *shake car.rla -over bg.iff*.

The car is composited over the background, but the sign and parking meter are obscured. We can fix this by using an outside command.

5   Type *shake car.rla -outside sign_mask.iff -over bg.iff*.

Now, the car is composited properly into the scene, that is, behind the sign and parking meter.

Okay, so you've had enough of command-line Shake. If you append -gui at the end of your commands, it will load them into the interface, allowing you to continue working in the Node workspace.

6   Type *shake car.rla -outside sign_mask.iff -over bg.iff -gui*.

This last set of commands is loaded into the GUI, and a tree is made for you.

Your tree should look like this:

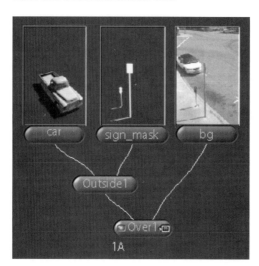

If you wanted, you could continue to work on this script in the GUI.

7   Quit Shake.

Launching Scripts from the Command Line

The most efficient way of doing gobs of rendering is by batch rendering a script, since you don't need to fire up the interface. All you need to do is to navigate to the location of one of your scripts and type *shake -v -exec my_cool_script.shk* (where *my_cool_script.shk* is a script that you create). The -exec command executes all FileOuts in the script. Each frame is rendered in turn, and since you typed -v, Shake shows you in the Terminal window which frame it is working on and how long each frame takes to render.

Welcome to the fabulous world of command-line Shake. You will no doubt be able to impress your friends with your newfound knowledge.

What You've Learned

- Command-line Shake enables you to do such things as render scripts, load images into a flipbook, and change image file formats—all without firing up the Shake interface.

- If you specify the fileout to be test.#.rgb, your file output will be test.0001.rgb.

- To see a complete list of commands, type *shake -help*.

A

Lesson Files	Appendix folder
Media	Object Passes folder
	macros folder
Start	LightStart.shk, MacroTree.shk, MultiLightStart.shk
Complete	MultipassFinish.shk
Bonus Files	AutoDOD Macro, ObjectColorChangeFinish.shk, Soften.shk
Time	approximately 1 hour
Goals	Combine multiple render passes from Maya into a single composite
	Create a macro node to automate repetition of multipass setup
	Add an external macro to Shake
	Adjust the properties of a 3D scene's lighting in Shake
	Uncover the parameters in Maya that are used to create multiple passes
	Discover the Z depth channel of a 3D image

Compositing Maya Renders in Shake

This appendix will introduce you to the power and flexibility of transferring multipass renders from Alias|Wavefront's Maya 3D into Shake for final compositing. If you do not have a Maya license, you can download a fully functional copy of Maya PLE (Personal Learning Edition) from www.aliaswavefront.com/en/products/maya/ple.

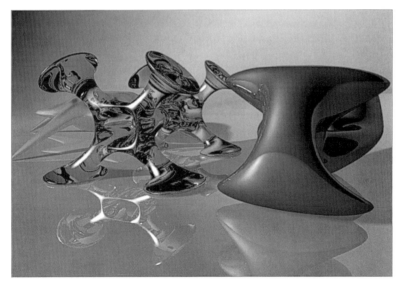

In a Maya-Shake workflow, you can change a 3D scene's lighting, shadows, and other effects without having to re-render.

Multipass as a Lifestyle

Imagine the following: You've just spent three weeks designing an amazing 3D animation for a primetime Thanksgiving Day television commercial. You waited another week for a render farm to finish calculating your scene's reflections, refractions, and all kinds of crazy experiments in radiosity. Finally, you see it and it's perfect; the penguin skates across the ice, morphs into a molten gold turkey, then smiles warmly as it slides all the way to the center of the family dinner table. It's just how you imagined it would be all those weeks ago when you first sketched the storyboards.

"The penguin's supposed to be blue." Those are the first words out of the CEO's mouth after viewing his commercial (*your* commercial) the day before it goes to air. So now, with at least another full week of rendering ahead of you to make the change, you're hosed.

At least you would be, if you'd failed to use Shake to pull together a multipass composite from elements rendered in Maya. By using Maya and Shake together, you can interactively change a 3D scene's lighting, object colors, reflections, shininess, shadows, focus effects, and more without needing to re-render. We'll look at the process here, starting with a very simplistic setup and moving to a scene with extremely fine control over elements. Oh, and we'll build a macro along the way.

> **NOTE ▶** For the following exercises, you'll be using pre-rendered image passes. For information on how to render the separate passes out of Maya, see the section "Rendering Out of Maya" later in this appendix.

A Multipass Lighting Composite

In this exercise, you'll composite a scene with a typical three-light setup—a key, a fill, and a rim light (also known as a back light). By taking advantage of a fairly simple Shake script, you can make significant changes to the scene lighting fairly easily. For this and the following sections, we'll be focusing on the key light. Later, we'll introduce the other two lights: fill and rim.

Compositing the Key Light

1　Start Shake.

2　Select File > Open Script.

3　Go to the Appendix/scripts folder on the DVD and load the **LightStart.shk** script.

You'll find four FileIn nodes, named **Key_Diff**, **Key_Spec**, **Key_Refl**, and **Key_Shad**.

4　Click on the left side of each of these clips to load them into the Viewer.

Each of these layers represents a different render pass of a light in our 3D scene of an Alien Bone Museum. This light is the key light, the light which is intended to bring out the main characteristics of the scene.

We've broken the scene up into four very common passes, though you can have other passes if it suits the scene being rendered. The **Key_Diff** file contains the diffuse information—basic color or shading. The **Key_Spec** contains the specular or "shiny bits" of the scene. These are the highlights on reflective and metallic objects, where the light seems to gather. The **Key_Refl** contains the scene's reflections. Finally the **Key_Shad** is a shadow pass, containing a grayscale "map" of where the shadows fall on the background.

5   Select **Key_Diff** and insert an IAdd from the Layers tab. Connect a noodle from **Key_Spec** to the second input knot of the IAdd. Double-click on IAdd1.

We've now combined the diffuse and specular passes.

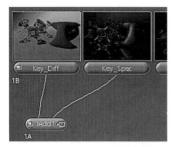

6   Add another IAdd from the Layer tab and connect **Key_Refl** to the second input.

7   Finally, connect an ISub from the Layers tab to IAdd2 and then connect **Key_Shad** to the second input of ISub1. View the final composite
by double-clicking on ISub1.

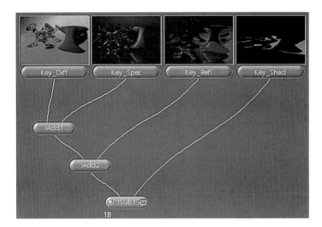

Subtraction is one method of applying the shadow, multiplying is
another. We'll try the multiply method next.

8   Ctrl-click on IMult from the Layers tab, replacing ISub1.

Something's not right. In order for the multiply to work, the shadow
pass matte must be inverted. Once inverted, wherever the matte is
white (no shadow), the image will remain at the same brightness;
wherever it's gray, the image will be darkened. (In Shake, white is
given the numeric value of 1. Any number multiplied by 1 is itself—
$3 \times 1 = 3$, $5 \times 1 = 5$, and so on. So wherever the inverted matte is
white (areas with no shadow), the image is unchanged. But if the
matte is darker (areas of shadow), the image is multiplied by a number less than 1, which lowers the brightness of those pixels and causes
a shadow. Think about it for a moment. It'll make sense.

9 Select **Key_Shad** (by clicking on the center of the node) and insert an
   Invert from the Color tab.

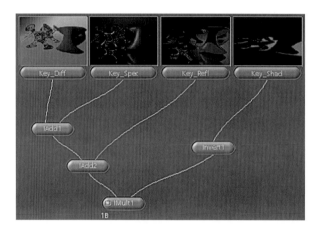

Looking at IMult1 you can now see the shadow, although it's much
more subtle than the one created via the subtraction method.

So what's the big deal? We've just put all the layers back together the way they would have been rendered out of Maya if we'd never made render passes. Where's the fun in that? Well, we need to add some controls to the interface before its true power becomes apparent.

10 Select **Key_Spec** and add to it a Brightness node from the Color tab. Rename Brightness1 to *SpecLevel*.

11 Also add separate Brightness nodes to **Key_Refl** and **Key_Shad,** renaming the new nodes *ReflLevel* and *ShadLevel*, respectively.

12 Select IMult1 and insert a Mult node from the Color tab. Rename Mult1 (*not* IMult1) to *MasterLevel*.

13 Save your script.

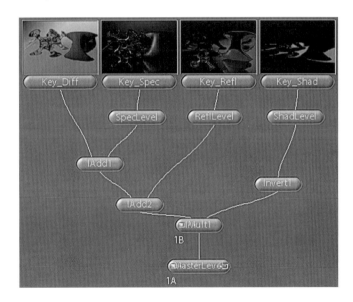

You now have controls for the amount of specularity, reflectivity, and shadow for the key light in our scene. We didn't add a Brightness node to **Key_Diff** because the diffuse pass is the basic building block of the image. We can use the MasterLevel node to control the overall intensity of the diffuse layer and use the other controls to decide how much of each other property is mixed back in.

This is all very nice, but there are several limitations to this composite tree. First, all the controls are adjusted in difference nodes, making it difficult to make quick tweaks. Each time you want to adjust a setting, you need to load that node's parameters into the Parameters1 tab. Second, this is only light one of three in this scene, so we'll need to rebuild the entire tree for each of the other lights. Well, lucky for you there's a single solution to both of those problems. It's a macro, and we're just about to build it.

Creating a Multipass Macro

Macros are user-created nodes that essentially "box up" a Shake script you've created so that no one can see the wiring (unless they really want to). It allows you to build your own node. As far as you're concerned, you might as well be looking at one of Shake's standard nodes, like an Over or a Mult. Think of a macro as a plug-in you can make without having to be a C++ programmer. The really great thing about macros is that they're very easy to create and very easy to reuse, and they conveniently put all your controls in one parameters tab.

Working with the MacroMaker

1   If something went tragically wrong with the last exercise, you can cheat by opening a previously prepared script. Select File > Open

Script, go to the Appendix/scripts folder, and load the **MacroTree.shk**
script. (Or simply continue with the script you saved in the previous
section.)

2   In the Node View, select all the nodes *except* the FileIn nodes—that is,
do *not* select **Key_Diff**, **Key_Spec**, **Key_Refl**, and **Key_Shad**.

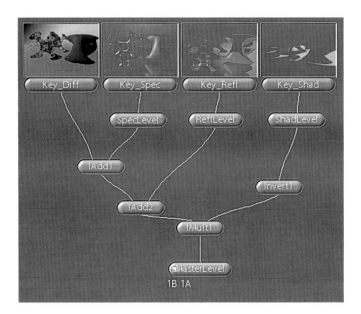

When creating a macro, you want to include only those parts of
your script that will always be part of the process. Since we're
building a macro to be used in all kinds of occasions, not *just*
with the four image files in our current scene, we leave these out
of the macro.

3 With all the nodes selected and your mouse over the Node View, press Shift-M (or choose Macro > Make Macro from the right-click menu in the Node View). This brings up the MacroMaker.

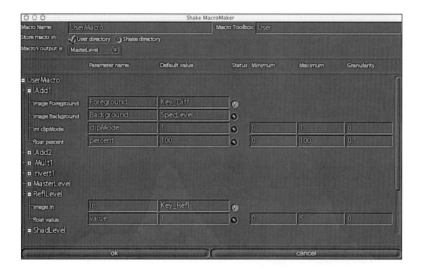

The MacroMaker is an incredibly easy way to create macros in Shake without having to geek out and type lines of code into a text editor (though once you start messing with macros, you might find yourself doing just that—and liking it). The only catch is that it's a one-way street. Once you click the OK button, you can't reopen the MacroMaker and make some quick changes. Your options are to edit the created macro outside of Shake in a text editor or repeat the process from the start. As a result, be sure and follow the next few steps carefully.

4 In the list of nodes you see under UserMacro, open the parameters of any nodes that are closed by clicking on the + to the left of the node's name.

We're about to choose from these lists of parameters the ones we want the user of our macro to be able to access. These will appear in our macro node's parameters window when we click the right side of the node. There are only a few controls that need to be edited; the rest can be fixed at a certain value and hidden.

Once you're done selecting from a given node which of its parameters will be visible in the final macro, click on the – to the left of the node name to close its parameters. When all the parameter groups are closed, you'll know you've finished selecting parameters.

5   In the Macro Name field, type *MultiLight*, and in the Macro Toolbox field, type *CG*.

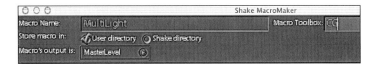

This sets the name of your macro to MultiLight and creates a new tab in the Tool tabs section called CG. If you had typed Layer instead, your macro would have ended up in the existing Layer tab.

Next to each parameter are six entry columns. Parameter name gives the name the user will see for that control in the parameters view. Default value is the value that the control will have when the macro is first added to a script. Status decides whether a parameter will show up in the final macro's parameters view; turning the "v" LED off will mean that the user will not be able to modify that control. The Minimum and Maximum fields decide the start and end range of the slider control associated with a parameter. A user can still numerically enter a number outside that range if she chooses. Granularity determines whether discreet numeric jumps will occur as the slider is moved.

6   In the IAdd1 section, rename the Foreground parameter *DiffuseIn*. Make sure the Status LED is illuminated. Make sure no other Status LEDs are illuminated in the IAdd1 section.

You've created an input knot on the macro called DiffuseIn. Don't worry about changing the default value; Shake will automatically treat this as a lonely knot just waiting to be connected to the greater scheme of things.

7   Close the IAdd1 section by clicking on the minus (–) to the left of its label.

8   There are no parameters in IAdd2, IMult1, or Invert1 that we want a user to access, so making sure there are no LEDs illuminated in the Status section of any of these nodes, close these sections as well.

9   In the MasterLevel parameters section, change the red parameter name field to *masterRed*, green to *masterGreen*, and blue to *masterBlue*. If you have previously adjusted the values in MasterLevel, you'll need to set the default values back to 1 in each of the three. Turn the LEDs on in the status section for all three of these parameters. Make sure no other LEDs are illuminated in the MasterLevel section, then close it up.

10 In ReflLevel, change the In parameter name to *ReflectIn* and the value parameter name to *reflection*. Make sure the default value for reflection is set to 1. Set both visibility LEDs to on. Close the section.

11 In ShadLevel, change the In parameter name to *ShadowIn* and the value parameter name to *shadow*. Make sure the default value for shadow is set to 1. Set both visibility LEDs to on. Close the section.

12 In SpecLevel, change the In parameter name to *SpecularIn* and the value parameter name to *specular*. Make sure the default value for specular is set to 1. Set both visibility LEDs to on. Close the section.

Now that all the sections are closed, you know that you have checked and set parameters for all nodes inside your macro.

13 To confirm that your settings are correct, check each macro section against the following screenshot:

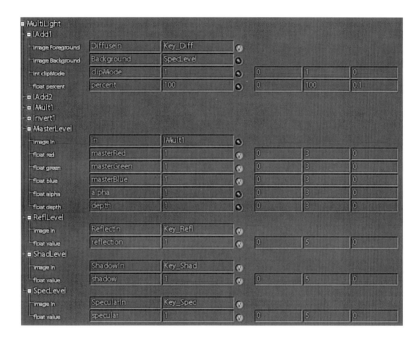

14 Make sure the Macro's output (towards the top left of the MacroMaker window) is set to MasterLevel, then click OK at the base of the window.

15 Look in the Tool tab section and you'll find a new tab called CG. In there, you'll find a single node selection button called MultiLight. Click on the button and your brand new macro is added to the Node View.

16 If you've made changes to your script other than creating the macro, save your work.

Using the MultiLight Macro

Having created your macro, it's time to use it. We'll now reapply the macro to our initial clips instead of the jungle of nodes we previously used.

1   Select File > Open Script.

2   Go to the Appendix/scripts folder and load the **LightStart.shk** script.

You'll find four FileIn nodes.

3   Select **Key_Diff** and insert the MultiLight node from the CG tab. Mouse over the first input knot of MultiLight1 (the knot to which **Key_Diff** is now attached) and read its name from the info line in the bottom-right corner of the screen. Make sure it is, in fact, the diffuse input. You should see MultiLight1.DiffuseIn written there.

You can change the order of the inputs on top of a macro, but doing so requires changing the macro script file via a text editor. This is relatively easy, but it's beyond the scope of this lesson. For more information, read the "How to Make a Macro" tutorial in the Shake documentation.

4   Drag a noodle from the output knot of **Key_Spec** and connect it to the SpecularIn knot of MultiLight1. Again, read the name of each knot from the info line to make sure you're connecting to the correct knot.

5   Connect **Key_Refl** and **Key_Shad** to their respective inputs.

You now have your macro connected and ready to use.

6   Double-click on MultiLight1.

7   Adjust the Parameters in Parameters1 and see the effect on the image in the Viewer.

8   Save your script.

Loading New Macros

You've now successfully applied your own macro. However, you may have noticed a few shortcomings. The interface for your parameters is quite messy, and instead of a nice color picker like the one in the regular Mult node, all you have are three plain color sliders—not an easy way to dynamically change the light's color. Worst of all, your new macro's button in the Tool tabs section is a plain line of text, not a pretty little graphic like the nodes that come with Shake.

To learn how to correct these problems, refer to the Shake User Guide. Or better yet, let's load a macro that's similar to the one you just built, but has a much nicer GUI layout and a pretty little graphic.

> **NOTE ►** The following tutorial assumes you created the macro in the previous exercise. If you didn't, you'll have to manually create some of the folders mentioned.

1   Close Shake and return to the Macintosh desktop.

2   In the Finder, navigate to the Appendix/macros folder on this book's DVD.

3   Copy all the files inside the macros folder to the same relative locations inside the nreal folder in your Home directory. If you're confident you can do this yourself, you can skip steps 4 through 13.

4   From the desktop, double-click on your hard drive's icon to open a new window.

5   Go to your Home directory inside your Users folder. Note: In the following figure, the Home directory is called Demo. Your Home directory will have the name of the account you logged into your machine with.

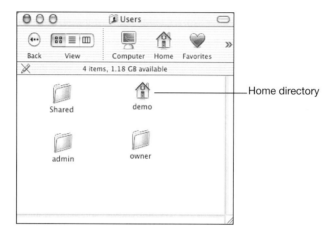

Home directory

6   Inside your Home directory, you'll find (among other things) a folder called nreal.

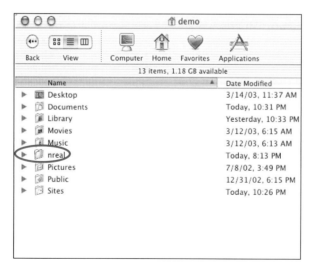

This is where all your personal settings for Shake are stored, including the autosaves of your scripts.

7   Double-click on the nreal folder.

Inside you'll find folders called autosave and include. Unless you've already added macros to your machine, you probably won't find an icons folder.

8   Create an icons folder by right-clicking in the window and choosing New Folder. Then click on the label Untitled Folder and rename it to *icons*.

9   Copy the contents from the icons folder on the DVD into your newly created icons folder. **CG.Multipass.nri** and **Transform.AutoDOD.nri** are the graphics for the Tool tab buttons; the files contained in ux provide GUI buttons inside the parameters view.

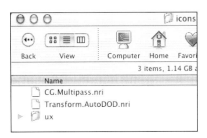

10   Double-click on the include folder (if you can't see it, you may have entered the icons folder, in which case click the Back button). Inside you'll find a startup folder.

11   Double-click on the startup folder. Inside you should find your newly created macro, **MultiLight.h**.

This is the file MacroMaker created, which contains the guts of your macro. If you'd like, you can open it up in a text editor and take a look.

12 Copy **AutoDOD.h** and **Multipass.h** from the DVD (see the following figure) into your startup folder (the one you just drilled down to from your Home directory).

13 Finally, copy **AutoDODUI.h** and **MultipassUI.h** from the DVD into the ui folder inside startup.

These ui files tell Shake how to draw the controls for your macro's interface.

Whew, aren't you glad that's all over? We needed to make sure all the files went to their correct locations, or Shake would be unable to see the macros on launch.

14 Relaunch Shake. You should now find a node called Multipass in your CG tab. You should also find a new node called AutoDOD in your Transform tab.

If you see an image of a mushroom cloud explosion either in the tabs where the button icons should be or inside the Parameters where radio buttons should be, you have not correctly added the icon files. Look back over steps 4 through 13 to see where good icons went bad.

The Multipass node is just a refined version of the MultiLight node we built earlier. The AutoDOD node is a bonus node, which tracks significant pixels in an image (when in Track mode), then sets the DOD of the image around the borders of the significant pixels (when in DOD mode). Note: AutoDOD works only with Shake version 3.0 or higher.

Compositing the Multipass Scene

It's now time to put it all together and create a dynamic scene with all three light passes. For the following exercise, we'll assume you've managed to get the Multipass node loaded into Shake, where it should be sitting patiently in the CG tab just waiting to be used. If for some reason files just didn't manage to go where they were supposed to, you can still use the MultiLight macro created earlier.

The Basic Composite

1   Select File > Open Script.

2   Go to the Appendix/scripts folder and load the **MultiLightStart.shk** script. You'll find twelve FileIn nodes, grouped into three sections, one for each light.

3   Select **Key_Diff** and insert a Multipass node from the CG tab (or use your MultiLight macro instead).

4   Attach **Key_Refl**, **Key_Spec**, and **Key_Shad** to their respective knots on Multipass1.

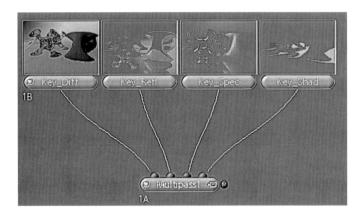

5   Select **Fill_Diff** and insert another Multipass node from the CD tab. Again, attach the reflective, specular, and shadow passes to their respective knots.

6   Repeat the process for the Rim passes.

7   Rename Multipass1 to *Key_light*, Multipass2 to *Fill_light*, and Multipass3 to *Rim_light*.

You now have all the passes composited together for each light.

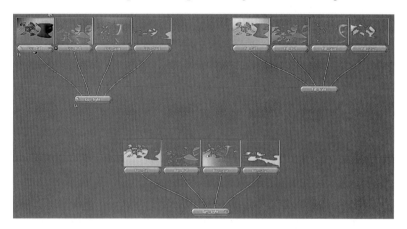

8   Select Key_light and insert an IAdd node from the Layers tab.

9   Connect the output of Fill_light to the second input of IAdd1.

10   Select IAdd1 and insert another IAdd node from the Layers tab.

11   Connect Rim_light to the second input of IAdd2.

12   Move to frame 45 in the Time Bar.

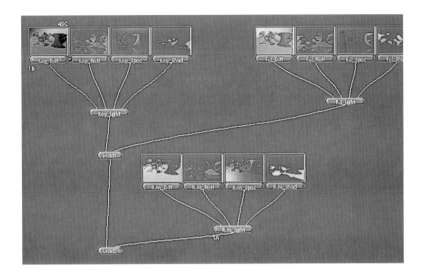

All the lights are now combined into one composite, with the output appearing at IAdd2. The following figure shows the three passes and the resulting composite. Unfortunately, everything looks extremely blown out. But that's OK, the fun's just beginning…

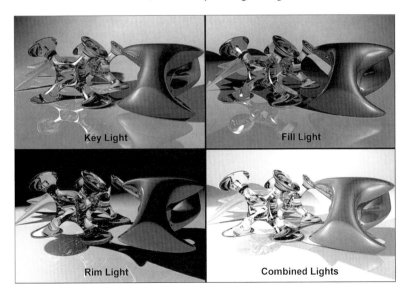

Adjusting the Lighting

1   Select Key_light and press Cmd-T to create a "tweaker box," which is simply a floating window that contains a node's parameters.

2   In the same fashion, create tweaker boxes for Fill_light and Rim_light.

3   Make sure IAdd2 is loaded into the Viewer, then with your mouse over the Viewer, press the spacebar to zoom the Viewer to full screen.

4   Position the Viewer and the tweaker boxes so everything fits nicely onscreen. You may need to resize the tweaker boxes to suit.

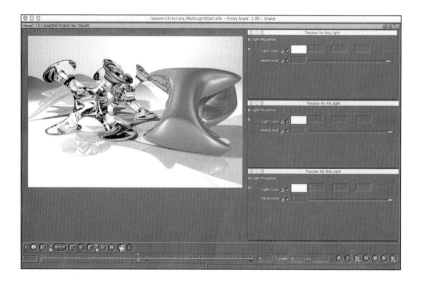

5   Drag the masterLevel sliders down to 0 for all three tweaker boxes.

Everything has now been plunged into pitch black. You only need to re-introduce the lighting as you need it.

6   Now, set the masterLevel of Key_light to 0.8.

The primary light of the scene is now illuminating the subjects of the shot. The shadows are a little too dramatic though. What's needed is a little diffuse lighting to lighten up the shadows.

7   Adjust the masterLevel of Fill_light to somewhere between 0.1 and 0.2.

That adds some general illumination to the shadows, but brings with it too much intensity in the speculars and an unwanted extra shadow. No problem—you can fix that.

8   Open the Light Properties section of Fill_light's tweaker and bring the specularLevel down to 0.3 and the shadowLevel down to 0.6.

Speculars are tamed, and the shadow is subtle.

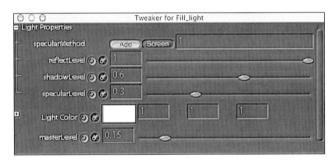

9   Adjust the masterLevel of Rim_light to around 0.25.

This introduces back lighting but also adds a shadow very close to the original key light, which confuses the image. Unlike true photography, where lighting shadows are a constant bane, computer-generated shadows can be turned on and off, so let's remove this unsightly blemish.

10 Open the Light Properties section of Rim_light's tweaker and set the shadowLevel to 0.

Starting to get it? With the multipass render from Maya, you're now able to make extremely powerful changes to the lighting dynamics of the scene. Maybe the key light is supposed to be flickering in time to spark sound effects. Use Shake's audio view to extract the sound's amplitude profile, then use it to adjust the masterLevel of Key_light. Perhaps things grow dark and ominous as the scene progresses. Slowly lower the Key_light and perhaps bring up the Fill. Changes to lighting that would have required days or weeks of re-rendering can be made in moments inside Shake if the render has been successfully broken down into passes.

Now, say the director comes into the room and suddenly decides that the scene needs to feel "lonelier." You manage to translate that into the more descriptive, "Make the scene look bluer." No problem. Simply click on the Key_light tweaker's color swatch and choose a more appropriate color. The other lights will still remain their same colors—only the illumination of the Key light will be colored.

Breaking Up Is Hard to Do

As an astute student of physics, light, and all things photoreal, you will have noticed that we've been adjusting the specularity, reflectivity, and so on for each *light* when these properties really belong to *objects*. An object's shininess (specularity) is intrinsic to its nature, not to the nature of the light that shines on it. What we have done here is attempt to fudge reality, not reproduce it. So for example, in the real world, light bounces all over the scene, creating a general illumination in shadows. We've attempted to "fake" this with the fill light in our scene. Since this light simulates a different effect entirely in the real world, we may not want it contributing extra specular shine to the objects in the scene.

Nonetheless, for full control, these objects need to be broken down into their own property passes. So rather than rendering out diffuse, specular, reflection, and shadow passes for each light, we could have rendered these passes out for each *object*. Further, we could also have rendered each of these object passes broken down by light.

For simplicity, we broke the scene down only by light (this is still a very powerful compositing technique when object properties are fixed). Breaking the scene up by object as well would have required 48 unique image files rendered out of Maya, as opposed to the current 12.

However, you'll see that we've also included an alpha channel for each *object* (you can find this footage in the folder footage/ObjectPasses), allowing you to modify the properties of a given object in the scene *without* having to make extra render passes. This is a very powerful and often overlooked way of adding object-level control with a minimal level of passes rendered out of Maya. With just the three alpha files provided we can turn our virtual penguin a nice shade of blue.

For extra credit:

1   FileIn to your existing scene from Appendix/footage/ObjectPasses/ the files **BoneCandyAlpha.iff**, **MartianKnuckleAlpha.iff**, and **StarFushAlpha.iff.**

2   Use these alpha channels to change only the BoneCandy object to green. (Hint: You may need to use the other alpha images to cut a hole in **BoneCandyAlpha.iff**, then use linked Mult nodes to complete the correction. **ObjectColorChangeFinish.shk** is a finished solution. If you're not sure what's going on, look at the text file **ObjectColorChangeExplained.txt** for an explanation (located in the scripts folder).

3   Soften the reflections on the floor, again using the alpha passes from the three objects. See **Soften.shk** for one possible solution.

Rendering Out of Maya

Maya has something called render layers, which allow you to choose which objects will be rendered together. These layers can be rendered out as separate beauty, diffuse, specular, and shadow passes. You should only use this system for the most simple of scenes. It doesn't handle reflections and tends to break down once scenes get more complex, especially where raytracing is involved.

Instead, you'll either need to create a MEL script to automate your multiple passes (or have someone make you one), hunt down a multipass plug-in from the Web, or simply save out separate scene files for each pass, turning on and off the visibility of objects and the properties of lights. Let's take a quick look at ways to render out these different passes from Maya.

Launch Maya 4.5 (or later) and open **AlienBones.mb** from the Appendix/Maya folder. (To download a free copy of Maya Personal Learning Edition go to www.aliawavefront.com/en/products/maya/ple.)

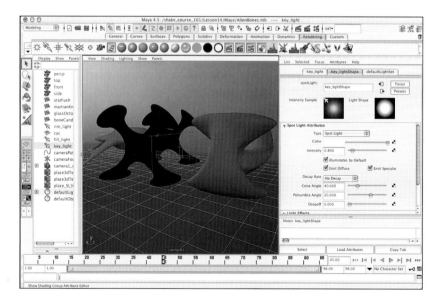

There are three main places you'll make modifications to your scene in order to render out separate passes: the render globals, light attributes, and object render stats. In the render globals, by turning off raytracing or lowering the Reflection slider to 0, you can render a pass with no reflections (this is sometimes preferable to attempting to render a scene with *only* reflections).

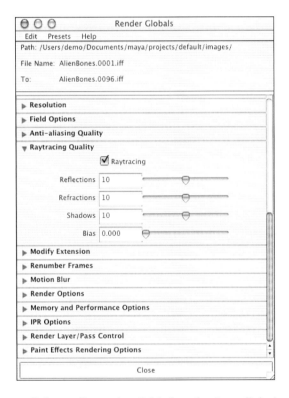

In light attributes (available by selecting a light in the Outliner and pressing Ctrl-A to bring up the attribute editor), you can render the diffuse and/or specular portions of the light. By turning off Emit Specular, leaving only Emit Diffuse, a diffuse pass can be rendered. To render only one light in a scene, simply set the other lights' Intensity settings to 0.

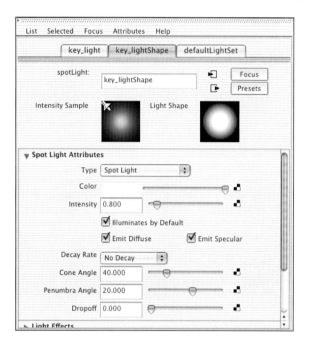

In an object's render stats (accessed via the main attributes tab of an object) are several check boxes that determine how an object responds to a scene. If you wanted to render each object as a separate pass, simply turn off Primary Visibility for all objects in the scene except for the one you're planning to render.

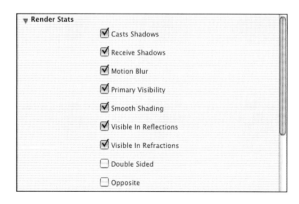

To create the shadow passes for the sample files, we turned all objects' Primary Visibility off, except for the background, cyc. Since all objects still had their Casts Shadows box checked, they cast shadows on the cyc, even though they themselves were not visible.

Finally, to achieve a shadow pass where the shadows were white on a black background, we set the lights' colors to black and their shadow colors to white. (You may also want to set your background's shader to Blinn and its color to pure white, fully diffuse.)

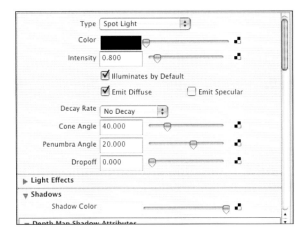

By combining these different settings, you can break down your render passes in myriad ways. You can save out several scenes from your original, one for each pass. If you find yourself using the same breakdown for most of your animations, it's probably time to write a MEL script to automatically break your passes down or find someone to write the MEL script for you.

More Maya–Shake Timesavers

In addition to multipass rendering, there are many other tricks you can do in a Maya-Shake workflow that are worth looking at quickly. The first of these is a collection of techniques leveraging the power of what's known as the Z buffer.

The Z Buffer

A major benefit of Maya's virtual 3D camera is that it can know things a real camera can't. One of those things is how far a pixel in the final image is from the Viewer.

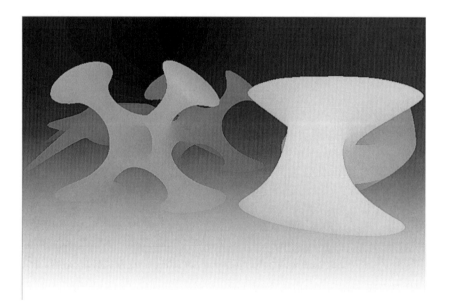

This information is stored in what's called a Z buffer, or the Z or depth channel. Different levels of gray mean that a given pixel is closer to the virtual camera or further away. Shake actually provides several ways to access the Z buffer recorded in an image. One of these is the Zcompose node, allowing you to composite one object over another based on their Z channels. The object closest to camera will be placed over the pixels of the image further away.

The problem is that the blending of foreground and background at edges that makes for a nice, anti-aliased composite simply doesn't work with a ZCompose. Each pixel in the depth matte can have only one depth value; it cannot simultaneously represent a partial mix of one pixel in the distance and another close-up (for example, see the aliased edges of our

BoneCandy object's Z channel in the following figure). Hence, you cannot blend the foreground and background together at object edges.

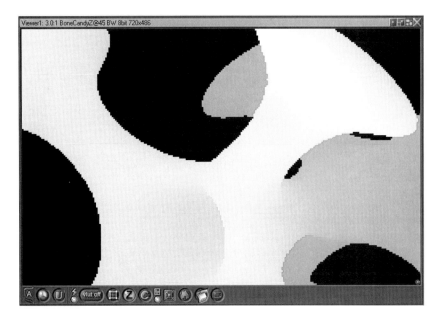

Z buffers do, however, come into their own when it comes to adding defocus effects, atmospheric color corrections, and so on. Although some of the edge alias issues still crop up, using a 16-bit Z channel out of Maya increases resolution and can provide a great deal of flexibility when it comes to applying depth-discriminating effects to an image.

Special Effects

There are a host of other special effects that can be created by combining Maya and Shake. Object shadows with varying penumbras can be created by simply animating the soft edge of a RotoShape fed into an IBlur. The same effect would take extra hours or days to render inside Maya with a raytraced area light. The softening caused by camera optics can be simulated, edge transparency can be modulated, highlights bloomed, particles blurred and treated—the list goes on. The more ways a scene is broken down in Maya, the more creative possibilities will be available inside Shake.

What You've Learned

- Combining multiple render passes from Maya in Shake allows many properties of a 3D scene to be tweaked without re-rendering.

- The MacroMaker can be used to quickly generate a macro node for frequent use.

- New macros can be added to Shake by placing their files in the appropriate folders inside your Home directory.

- By adjusting the properties of objects and lights in Maya, different passes can be set up and rendered.

- The Z channel of a 3D image provides information on how far pixels are from the camera.

Keyboard Shortcuts

Cmd-T	Opens a parameter's tweaker box for a given node

Appendix **B**

Apple's Digital Production Platform: An Integrated Workflow

Apple has developed a line of professional film, video, and audio production applications that, taken together, give professionals an affordable high-performance, integrated digital production platform. Each product is recognized as an industry standard in its respective field. When used together, they form a complete pipeline from content creation to delivery.

Here's a brief overview of how the four keystone applications—Final Cut Pro, Shake, Logic, and DVD Studio Pro—work together in a variety of standard production workflows.

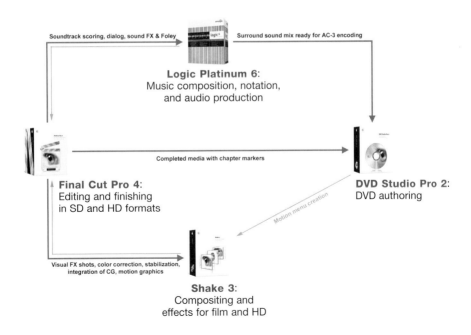

Soundtrack scoring, dialog, sound FX & Foley · Surround sound mix ready for AC-3 encoding

Logic Platinum 6:
Music composition, notation, and audio production

Completed media with chapter markers

Final Cut Pro 4:
Editing and finishing
in SD and HD formats

DVD Studio Pro 2:
DVD authoring

Motion menu creation

Visual FX shots, color correction, stabilization,
integration of CG, motion graphics

Shake 3:
Compositing and
effects for film and HD

Final Cut Pro

Final Cut Pro is a fully scalable nonlinear editing system designed to work with all standard video formats from DV to High Definition. More than just an editing application, Final Cut Pro lets you easily add filters and transitions to clips and play them in real time using an effects engine known as RT Extreme. Real-time color correction, customizable keyboard commands, dynamic and asymmetric trimming, broadcast video scopes, and support for multichannel audio editing, mixing, and output are a few of the features that make Final Cut Pro a great tool for serious editors.

Four integrated applications are also included with Final Cut Pro: LiveType, a powerful title generation tool; Soundtrack, an audio creation application that lets you build original, high-quality musical scores for your video; Cinema Tools, a sophisticated relational database that lets you shoot and finish on film and 24P (HD) while using Final Cut Pro for your editing; and Compressor, a high-speed encoding application that offers a variety of distribution formats including MPEG-4 and MPEG-2.

In the Pipeline

For more robust compositing, special-effects plates can be exported from Final Cut Pro and layered and manipulated in Shake. Audio elements in need of additional processing and mixing can be exported to Logic Audio for sweetening, and rough scores created in Soundtrack can be enhanced by professional composers in Logic. When completed, all treated media can be imported to DVD Studio Pro for professional DVD authoring.

Shake

Shake is a high-end compositing system used to create visual effects for award-winning broadcast commercials and box-office–champion feature films like *The Lord of the Rings* and *The Matrix*. Shake is typically used for combining elements from multiple sources into a single image, creating the illusion that everything was filmed "in camera." These elements include 3D animation, particles, procedural painting, and live-action plates.

Unlike the timeline-based compositing in Final Cut Pro, Shake uses a node-based architecture. Each operator is a discrete unit that can be plugged into other operators in an incredibly flexible, nonlinear fashion, creating a detailed process tree that leads to the final composited shot. Shake also includes two industry-standard keyers for greenscreen and bluescreen work—Photron's Primatte and Framestore/CFC's Keylight—along with numerous precise color correction tools.

In the Pipeline

Any shot that requires multilayered visual effects is a job for Shake. One of the most common shots to be sent to Shake is a bluescreen or greenscreen. While Final Cut Pro has built-in keyers, Shake includes far more sophisticated keying techniques based on color difference and 3D color space technology.

Another common use for Shake is footage stabilization and match moving. Shake can stabilize position, scale, rotation, and perspective, salvaging shaky footage that would otherwise be unusable. Using the same technology, Shake can match the motion in a camera shot so that composited elements seem to "belong" in the scene.

Logic

Logic Platinum is a complete virtual recording studio used to create and edit music sound tracks, dialogue, and sound effects as well as to mix and master final audio files (including surround sound). Logic contains a fully scalable mixing console, dozens of effects processors, and the option to add Emagic's world-class software-based synthesizers as virtual instruments. In addition, it is designed with advanced MIDI handling to access external synthesizers, keyboards, and other MIDI-enabled instruments. The software contained in Logic rivals some of the most sophisticated hardware-based recording studios in the world in both audio quality and creative control.

In the Pipeline

Logic works simultaneously with SMPTE timecode, meaning that sounds can be positioned based on events in time, rather than on musical beats and bars. This makes it ideal for work on film and video sound tracks.

Video can be previewed in a floating window or viewed as a thumbnail track in order to make precise matches to cuts and significant events in the narrative.

The most obvious use for Logic is in the creation of a musical score. Logic is also indispensable for working with nonmusical elements in a project, cleaning up inaudible dialogue or restoring room ambiance in scenes where overdubbed dialogue had replaced the original audio.

In addition, Surround sound mixing is directly incorporated into Logic. DVD Studio Pro includes a Dolby AC3 surround sound encoding system, which can take Logic output tracks and encode them for DVD distribution.

DVD Studio Pro

DVD Studio Pro is a complete DVD authoring platform. It takes video, audio, and image content and combines them into an interactive menu-driven DVD. This can include motion menus, chapter and title access, special features, and slide shows. Basically, anything you've seen in a commercial DVD product can be created using DVD Studio Pro. The application also includes Compressor, a powerful software-based MPEG2 encoding tool, as well as the AC3 encoder mentioned in the Logic section above.

In the Pipeline

DVD Studio Pro is obviously the last step in a production workflow, where media content is assembled for delivery. The DVD authoring may be one of several delivery streams coming from the Final Cut Pro media; others may include video mastering, Web streaming, or even external film edits. One handy feature of Final Cut Pro is its ability to create and export chapter markers for use in DVD Studio Pro.

Other ways DVD Studio Pro and Final Cut Pro can work together include the creation of 4:3 pan-and-scan versions of a 16:9 piece, preparation of multiple-angle clips, and development of complex motion menus. Shake can be used for motion menus, its nonlinear workflow making it ideal for quickly generating alternate motion selection and rollover button states.

Glossary

3:2 pulldown A technique to convert film footage to video footage and back again.

\#

A

AIFF file Short for Audio Interchange File Format, an 8-bit sound file format developed by Apple.

alpha channel In color images, the fourth channel after the red, green, and blue channels. In black-and-white images, the second channel after the luminance channel.

Audio Panel A tool used to read in AIFF or WAV files, mix them together, extract animation curves based on the audio frequency, and manipulate the timing of the sound.

B

blue screen Images are shot in front of an evenly lit, bright, pure blue background. The compositing process then replaces all the blue in the picture with another image.

C

Channel Viewer Toggles between the full color image and the alpha channel.

chromakey Electronically matting or inserting an image from one camera into the picture produced by another. The subject to be inserted is shot against a solid color background, and signals from the two sources are then merged.

color correction Any process that alters the perceived color of an image.

color matching Matching the color of shot to another.

Color Picker A tool that allows you to sample colors from the Viewer and transfer the color settings to applicable parameters.

compositing Creating an image by combining two or more images.

concatenation The process of mathematically combining multiple color corrections into one.

Curve Editor A tool that allows you to create, see, and modify keyframes as well as animation curves and audio waveforms.

D
F

dustbusting The process of painting dirt off of an image.

File Browser An interactive browser to track files or to navigate through the network to load or write scripts, images, lookup files, and expressions.

FileIn Node used to read images into Shake.

FileOut Node used to save images.

filter A function that takes an image and transforms it in some manner, such as a blur filter.

flipbook A RAM-based image player that loads a clip into memory so that it can be played back in real time.

Frame stroke mode Used to paint only on the current frame.

function See *nodes*.

G

garbage matte A matte that removes unwanted objects from an image.

Global parameters Parameters that affect the behavior of your entire effect setup.

I

interlace The manner in which a television picture is composed, scanning alternate lines of two different video fields to create one frame every $\frac{1}{30}$ of a second in NTSC.

Interpolate stroke mode Interpolates brush strokes between chosen frames.

K

keyframe A value set at various frames of an animation. Keyframes transition from one to another over time.

knot A point on an animation curve or shape.

Kodak Cineon A 10-bit logarithmic file format that uses an efficient color compression scheme based on the idea that the human eye is more sensitive to low- and mid-tones than to highlights.

M

mask An image or a part of an image usually used to limit or constrain an effect.

matte An image that controls the opacity of another image.

motion tracking A technique that involves selecting a particular region of an image and analyzing its motion over time.

multi-pass compositing The process of separating scenes into multiple layers, allowing flexibility in the manipulation and adjustment of the various layers.

nodes The image manipulation commands used in Shake.

N

Node workspace The Shake workspace where clips and functions, as represented by nodes, are combined and connected into a process tree.

noodle A line connecting nodes on a process tree.

NTSC National Television Standards Committee, which developed the color transmission system used in the U.S. Consists of 525 lines scanned at 30 frames per second.

on-the-fly proxy A proxy that is generated only when needed and discarded when your disk is full.

O

PAL Phase Alternation by Line. The color television system used by many European countries. Consists of 625 lines scanned at a rate of 25 frames per second.

P

penumbra The soft edge of a shadow.

Parameters workspace The Shake workspace where parameters for a node are adjusted.

Persist stroke mode Brush strokes persist from frame to frame in this mode.

premultiplication Images have their RGB channels multiplied by their alpha channels.

Primatte A technology used to extract a single color background from an image and create a transparency matte that allows the user to put the extracted foreground onto a different background.

process tree A treelike structure comprising interconnected images and processes such as color corrections, layering commands, and keying functions, among others.

proxy A lower-resolution copy that you substitute for your high-resolution images.

proxy button Used to activate the use of proxy resolutions.

proxy ratio Determines the size relationship of the proxy to the base file.

R

radiosity The use of intensive computer calculations to simulate light bouncing off multiple objects, losing energy and changing color as part of the light absorption of a reflective surface. Scenes featuring radiosity take an extremely long time to render.

reference pattern The inner box of a tracker. It defines a small pattern that will be searched for in subsequent frames.

refraction The process of light "bending" as it travels through objects with densities different from air, such as glass or water.

render The conversion of an image into a fully formed, 3D image.

render pass A single image rendered from a 3D scene, containing only part of the scene's properties. A Z-buffer channel included with an image is sometimes referred to as a *depth pass*.

resolution The quality of an image.

RGB channel The combination of the red, green, and blue channels of an image.

rotoscoping A frame-by-frame, hand-painting technique to create imagery over time.

rotoshaping A frame-by-frame, shape-drawing technique to create animated shapes over time.

script A text file that contains all of the information about your process tree. The script can be loaded into the interface for further modification.

scrub The action of shuttling an image sequence back and forth.

search region The outer box of a tracker, which should be the maximum amount your tracking point will move between frames.

thumbnail A small, "thumbnail-sized" version of an image.

Time Bar A display of a time range.

Tool tabs All the various Shake tools are conveniently located in the Tool tabs window.

tracker A node that analyzes the motion of a clip.

track point The center cross in a tracker. It represents the position of the motion track.

transform control A control that allows you manipulate an image using parameters such as pan, scale, and rotate.

Viewer A display tool for viewing images.

WAV A sound file format developed by Microsoft and IBM.

Z buffer A grayscale image sometimes contained in a rendered 3D image file representing the distance of each pixel in the rendered image from the virtual camera. Light pixels in the Z buffer are further away from the camera than darker pixels, or vice versa. Can be used for modulating the strength of effects such as Zdefocus and Zblur, modulating contrast, or even compositing separate images based on their depth relationships.

Index

thumbnails
blob clips, 104–105
described, 435
hiding, 105
keyboard shortcuts, 120
RotoShapes, 115
transparency, 104
.tif extension, 62
TIFF files, 62
Time Bar
described, 103–104, 435
scrolling through
animation with, 136
viewing composites, 141
Time Shift parameter, 241
Time View tab, 20
timecode, 236
timeline, 20
timeRange parameter, 46, 102
TimeView tab, 330–333
timing, 241, 321–323
title bar functions, 21–24
title bar information, 24
Toggle Fill/No Fill button, 193
Toggle Path button, 193
tolerance parameters, 377–378
Tool tabs
described, 14–16, 435
keyboard shortcuts, 65
Track buttons, 290, 351
Track Gain parameter, 242
track point, 287, 349, 435
tracker
adjusting, 377–379
described, 435
positioning, 286–290
stopping, 290
Tracker node, 192, 285, 346
tracking, 345–379
applying tracking data,
367–371

building example, 351–355
described, 345
four-point, 362–377
image quality, 350
keyframes, 379
motion, 284–292, 433
offset, 355–358
one-point, 346–361
reverse, 358
viewing clips for, 346–347
watch example, 364–366
tracking, motion, 284–292
tracking curve, 289–292
trackRange parameter,
289–290
tracks
accuracy of, 377–379
audio, 241
averaging, 358–361
choosing, 290–292
slipping, 241
trackType parameter, 290–291,
353
training centers, 7
transform controls
centering, 181
described, 435
parent-child relationships,
179–181
right mouse on, 179–181
shapes, 175, 186, 193
transforming images, 108–112
transparency
color, 248
foreground, 249
keying operations and, 255
matte, 248
removing, 249
thumbnails, 104
trees. *See* process trees; scripts
tutorials, Shake Help, 6

U
ui folder, 416
Ultimate keyer, 245
Undo button, 130
Undo feature, 22, 130, 152
undo/redo buttons, 22
undo shortcuts, 39
Unix commands, 382–384, 387
Unix systems, 382–383
Unlock Tangents button, 193
Update buttons, 22–23
Update modes, 32–34, 82
useProxy parameters, 200–207
UserMacro, 408

V
-v flag, 390
variables, local, 336–337
video fields, 228–236
video footage, 251–254
video frames. *See* frames
video functions, 236–237
VideoSafe function, 236
Viewer
AutoKey button, 113,
130–131
Channel, 30–31
command-line functions,
386
comparing images, 34–37
described, 435
general controls, 29–32
keyboard shortcuts, 40
loading nodes into, 46
moving images in, 109
On-Screen controls,
108–112
RotoShape controls, 193
update modes, 32–34
viewing nodes in, 45–46
working with, 29–38
zooming in, 30, 211